Editor
Dona Herweck Rice

Editorial Project Manager
Dona Herweck Rice

Editor-in-Chief
Sharon Coan, M.S. Ed.

Illustrator
Sue Fullam

Cover Artist
Barb Lorseyedi

Art Coordinator
Kevin Barnes

Imaging
Alfred Lau
Rosa C. See

Product Manager
Phil Garcia

Publishers
Rachelle Cracchiolo, M.S. Ed.
Mary Dupuy Smith, M.S. Ed.

Comprehension & Critical Thinking

LEVEL 2

Includes Document-Based Questions

Author

Debra J. Housel, M.S. Ed.

Reading passages provided by *TIME For Kids* magazine.

Teacher Created Materials, Inc.
6421 Industry Way
Westminster, CA 92683
www.teachercreated.com
ISBN-0-7439-3372-9
©2002 Teacher Created Materials, Inc.
Reprinted, 2004
Made in U.S.A.

Table of Contents

Introduction

Comprehension is the primary goal of any reading task. Students who comprehend what they read have more opportunities in life as well as better test performance. Through the use of interesting grade-level nonfiction passages followed by exercises that require vital reading and thinking skills, *Comprehension and Critical Thinking* will help you to develop confident readers who can demonstrate their knowledge on standardized tests. In addition, you will promote the comprehension necessary to form the basis for a lifetime of learning.

The articles in *Comprehension and Critical Thinking* present facts about the contemporary world as well as the past. A document-based question for each passage gives your students practice in the newest trend in standardized testing. The students respond to a critical-thinking question based on the information gleaned from a given document (often a picture). This document is related to the passage it accompanies. Document-based questions show a student's ability to apply prior knowledge and his or her capacity to transfer knowledge to a new situation.

The activities are time efficient, allowing students to practice these skills every week. To yield the best results, such practice must begin at the start of the school year.

Students will need to use test-taking skills and strategies throughout their lives. The exercises in *Comprehension and Critical Thinking* will guide your students to become better readers *and* test-takers. After practicing the exercises in this book, you will be pleased with your students' comprehension performance, not only on standardized tests, but with *any* expository text they encounter—within the classroom and beyond its walls.

Readability

All of the passages have a 2.0-2.9 reading level based on the Flesch Kincaid Readability Formula. This formula determines a readability level by calculating the number of words, syllables, and sentences. The passages are presented in order of increasing difficulty.

Preparing Students to Read Nonfiction Text

One of the best ways to prepare students to read expository text is to read a short selection aloud to them daily. Reading expository text aloud is critical to developing your students' ability to read it themselves. Since making predictions is another way to make students tap into their prior knowledge, read the beginning of a passage, then stop, and ask them to predict what might occur next. Do this at several points throughout your reading of the text. By doing this, over time you will find that your students' ability to make accurate predictions greatly increases.

Of course, talking about nonfiction concepts is also very important. Remember, however, that discussion can never replace reading aloud because people rarely speak using the vocabulary and complex sentence structures of written language.

Questions help students, especially struggling readers, to focus on what's important in a text. Also, remember the significance of wait time. Research has shown that the amount of time an educator waits for a student to answer after posing a question has a critical effect on learning. So after you ask a student a question, silently count to five (or ten if you have a student who struggles to get his or her thoughts into words) before giving any additional prompts or redirecting the question to another student.

Introduction (cont.)

Bloom's Taxonomy

The questions that follow each passage in *Comprehension and Critical Thinking* assess all levels of learning by following Bloom's Taxonomy, a six-level classification system for comprehension questions devised by Benjamin Bloom in 1956. The questions that follow each passage are always presented in order, progressing from knowledge to evaluation.

The skills listed for each level are essential to keep in mind when teaching comprehension to assure that your students reach the higher levels of thinking. Use this classification to form your own questions whenever your students listen to or read material.

Level 1: Knowledge—Students recall information or find requested information in an article. They show memory of dates, events, places, people, and main ideas.

Level 2: Comprehension—Students understand information. This means that they can find information that is stated in a different way than the question. It also means students can rephrase or restate information in their own words.

Level 3: Application—Students apply their knowledge to a specific situation. They may be asked to do something new with the knowledge.

Level 4: Analysis—Students break things into their component parts and examine those parts. They notice patterns in information.

Level 5: Synthesis—Students do something new with the information. They pull knowledge together to create new ideas. They generalize, predict, plan, and draw conclusions.

Level 6: Evaluation—Students make judgments and assess value. They form an opinion and defend it. They can also understand another person's viewpoint.

Practice Suggestions: Multiple Choice Questions

Do the first three passages and related questions with the whole class. These passages have the most challenging reading level (2.9) because you will be doing them together. Demonstrate your own metacognitive processes by thinking aloud about how to figure out an answer. This means that you essentially tell your students your thoughts as they come to you. For example, suppose the question is the following: "In a national park, bears a) roam free, b) stay in cages, or c) get caught in traps." Tell the students all your thoughts as they occur to you, for example: "Well, the article was about bears living in national parks. It didn't mention that they stay in cages. They probably only do that in zoos or circuses. So I'll get rid of that choice. That leaves me with the choices 'roam free' or 'get caught in traps.' Let me look back at the article and see what it says about traps. (Refer to the article.) I don't see anything about traps in the passage. And I do see that it says that in national parks the bears are safe. That means they're safe from traps, which are dangerous. So I'm going to select a) roam free."

Introduction *(cont.)*

Short-Answer Questions

The short-answer question for each passage is evaluative—the highest level of Bloom's Taxonomy. It is basically an opinion statement with no definitive right answer. The child is asked to take a stance and defend it. While there is no correct response, it is critical to show them how to support their opinions using facts and logic. Show them a format for response—state their opinion followed by the word "because" and a reason. For example: I do not think that whales should be kept at sea parks because they are wild animals and don't want to be there. They want to be in the ocean with their friends. *Do not award credit unless the child adequately supports his or her conclusion.* Before passing back the practice papers, make note of two children who had opposing opinions. Then, during the discussion, call on each of these students to read his or her short-answer response to the class. (If all the children drew the same conclusion, come up with support for the opposing one yourself.)

Document-based Questions

It is especially important to guide your students in how to understand, interpret, and respond to the document-based questions. For these questions, in order to formulate a response the students will have to rely on their prior knowledge and common sense in addition to the information provided in the document. Again, the best way to teach this is to demonstrate through thinking aloud how to figure out an answer. Since these questions are usually interpretive, you can allow for some variation in student responses.

The more your students practice, the more competent and confident they will become. Plan to have the class do every exercise in *Comprehension and Critical Thinking*. If you have some students who cannot read the articles independently, allow them to read with a partner, then work through the comprehension questions alone. Eventually all students must practice reading and answering the questions independently. Move to this stage as soon as possible. For the most effective practice sessions, follow these steps:

1. Have the students read the text silently and answer the questions.

2. Have the students exchange papers to correct each other's multiple choice section.

3. Collect all the papers to score the short-answer question and the document-based question portion.

4. Return the papers to their owners and discuss how the students determined their answers.

5. Refer to the exact wording in the passage.

6. Point out how students had to use their background knowledge to answer certain questions.

7. Discuss how a child should explain his or her stance in each short-answer question.

8. Discuss the document-based question thoroughly.

Introduction (cont.)

Scoring the Practice Passages

With the students, use the "number correct" approach to scoring the practice passages, especially since this coincides with the student achievement graph on page 109. However, for your own records and to share with the parents, you may want to keep track of numeric scores for each student. If you choose to do this, do not write the numeric score on the paper.

To generate a numeric score, follow these guidelines:

Multiple choice questions (6)	10 points each	60 points
Short-answer question (1)	15 points	15 points
Document-based question (1)	25 points	25 points
Total		100 points

Standardized Test Success

One of the key objectives of *Comprehension and Critical Thinking* is to prepare your students to get the best possible scores on the reading portion of standardized tests. A student's ability to do well on traditional standardized tests in comprehension requires these factors:

- a large vocabulary
- test-taking skills
- the ability to cope with stress effectively

Test-taking Skills

Every student in your class needs instruction in test-taking skills. Even fluent readers and logical thinkers will perform better on standardized tests if you provide instruction in the following areas:

Understanding the question: Teach students to break down the question to figure out what is really being asked of them. This book will prepare them for the kinds of questions they will encounter on standardized tests.

Concentrating on just what the text says: Show students how to restrict their response to just what is asked. When you go over the practice passages, ask your students to show where they found the correct response *in the text*.

Ruling out distracters in multiple choice answers: Teach students to look for the key words in a question and look for those specific words to find the information in the text. They also need to know that they may have to look for synonyms for the key words.

Maintaining concentration: Use classroom time to practice this in advance. Reward students for maintaining concentration. Explain to them the purpose of this practice and the reason why concentration is so essential.

Introduction (cont.)

Practice environmental conditions throughout the year in order to acclimate your students to the testing environment. For example, if your students' desks are usually together, have students move them apart whenever you practice so it won't feel strange on the test day.

Some other ideas for "setting the stage" whenever you practice include the following:

- Put a "Testing—Do Not Disturb" sign on the door.

- Require no talking, active listening, and following directions during practice sessions.

- Provide a small strip of construction paper for each student to use as a marker.

- Give each student two sharpened pencils and have a back-up supply handy. Tell the students to raise a broken pencil, and you will immediately provide them with a new one.

Coping with Stress

Teach students to recognize their apprehension and other stressful feelings associated with testing. Give students some suggestions for handling stress, such as taking a deep breath and stretching.

At the beginning of the school year start talking about good habits like getting enough rest, having a good breakfast, and daily exercise. Enlist parental support by sending home a letter encouraging parents to start these good habits right away.

Remember to let students stretch and move around between tests. Provide a physical release by running in place or playing "Simon Says" as a stress-buster during practice sessions throughout the year as well as on the test day.

Build confidence throughout the school year by using the practice passages in this book. Do not include the passage scores in the students' class grades. Instead, encourage your students by having them complete the Student Achievement Graph on page 109, showing how many questions they answered correctly for each practice passage. Seeing their scores improve or stay consistently high over time will provide encouragement and motivation.

On the test day, promote a relaxed, positive outlook. Tell your students to visualize doing really well. Remind them that since they have practiced so much, they are thoroughly prepared.

Teaching Nonfiction Comprehension Skills

Nonfiction comprehension encompasses many skills that develop with a lot of practice. The following information offers you a brief overview of how to teach the crucial skills of recognizing text structure, visualizing, summarizing, and learning new vocabulary. This information is designed for your use with other classroom materials, not the practice passages in *Comprehension and Critical Thinking*.

Introduction *(cont.)*

You will find many of these skills in scope-and-sequence charts and standards for reading comprehension:

- recognizes stated main idea
- identifies details
- determines sequence
- recalls details
- labels parts
- summarizes
- identifies time sequence
- describes character
- retells information in own words
- classifies, sorts into categories
- compares and contrasts
- makes generalizations
- draws conclusions
- recognizes text organization
- predicts outcome and consequences
- experiences an emotional reaction to a text
- recognizes facts
- applies information to a new situation

Typical Comprehension Questions

Teaching the typical kinds of standardized test questions gives students an anticipation framework and helps them learn how to comprehend what they read. It also boosts their test scores. The questions generally found on standardized reading comprehension tests are as follows:

Facts—questions based on exactly what the text states: who, what, when, where, why, and how many

Sequence—questions based on order: what happened first, last, and in between

Conditions—questions asking students to compare, contrast, and find the similarities and differences

Summarizing—questions that require students to restate, paraphrase, choose main ideas, conclude, and select a title

Vocabulary—questions based on word meaning, synonyms and antonyms, proper nouns, words in context, technical words, geographical words, and unusual adjectives

Outcomes—questions that ask readers to draw upon their own experiences or prior knowledge, which means that students must understand cause and effect, consequences, and implications

Opinion—questions that ask the author's intent and require the use of inferencing skills

Document-based—questions that require students to analyze information from a source document to draw a conclusion or form an opinion

Introduction *(cont.)*

Teaching Text Structure

Students lacking in knowledge of text structure are at a distinct disadvantage; yet this skill is sometimes overlooked in instruction. When referring to a piece to locate information to answer a question, understanding structure allows students to locate quickly the right area in which to look. Students also need to understand text structure in order to make predictions and improve overall comprehension.

Some children have been so immersed in print that they have a natural understanding of structure. For instance, they realize that the first sentence of a paragraph often contains the main idea, followed by details about that idea. But many students need direct instruction in text structure. The first step in this process is making certain that students know the way that authors typically present ideas in writing. This knowledge is a major asset for students.

Transitional paragraphs join together two paragraphs to make the writing flow. Most transitional paragraphs do not have a main idea. In all other paragraph types, there is a main idea, even if it is not stated. In the following examples the main idea is italicized. In order of frequency, the four types of expository paragraph structures are as follows:

1. **The main idea is often the first sentence of a paragraph. The rest of the paragraph provides the supporting details.**

   Clara Barton, known as America's first nurse, was a brave and devoted humanitarian. While caring for others, she was shot at, got frostbitten fingers, and burned her hands. She had severe laryngitis twice and almost lost her eyesight. Yet she continued to care for the sick and injured until she died at the age of 91.

2. **The main idea may fall in the center of the paragraph, surrounded on both sides by details.**

   The coral have created a reef where more than 200 kinds of birds and about 1,500 types of fish live. *In fact, Australia's Great Barrier Reef provides a home for many interesting animals.* These include sea turtles, giant clams, crabs, and crown-of-thorns starfish.

3. **The main idea comes at the end of the paragraph as a summary of the details that came before.**

   Each year Antarctica spends six months in darkness, from mid March to mid September. The continent is covered year-round by ice, which causes sunlight to reflect off its surface. It never really warms up. In fact, the coldest temperature ever recorded was in Antarctica. *Antarctica has one of the harshest environments in the world.*

4. **The main idea is not stated in the paragraph and must be inferred from the details given. This paragraph structure is the most challenging for primary students.**

   The biggest sea horse ever found was over a foot long. Large sea horses live along the coasts of New Zealand, Australia, and California. Smaller sea horses live off the coast of Florida, in the Caribbean Sea, and in the Gulf of Mexico. The smallest adult sea horse ever found was only one-half inch long!

   In this example, the implied main idea is that sea horses' sizes vary based on where they live.

Introduction *(cont.)*

Some other activities that will help your students understand text structure include the following:

Color code: While reading text, have your students use different colored pencils or highlighters to color code important elements such as the main idea (red), supporting details (yellow), causes (green) and effects (purple), facts (blue) and opinions (orange). When they have finished, ask them to describe the paragraph's structure in their own words.

Search the text: Teach students to identify the key words in a question and look specifically for those words in the passage. Then, when you discuss a comprehension question with the students, ask them, "Which words will you look for in the text to find the answer? If you can't find the words, can you find synonyms? Where will you look for the words?"

Signal words: There are specific words used in text that indicate, or signal, that the text has a cause and effect, sequence, or comparison structure. Teaching your students these words will greatly improve their ability to detect text structure and increase their comprehension.

These Signal Words	Indicate
since, because, caused by, as a result, before and after, so, this led to, if/then, reasons, brought about, so that, when/then, that's why	cause and effect The answer to **"Why did it happen?"** is a cause. The answer to **"What happened?"** is an effect.
first, second, third, next, then, after, before, last, later, since then, now, while, meanwhile, at the same time, finally, when, at last, in the end, since that time, following, on (date), at (time)	sequence
but, even if, even though, although, however, instead, not only, unless, yet, on the other hand, either/or, as well as, "–er" and "–st" words (such as better, best, shorter, tallest, bigger, smallest, most, worst)	compare/contrast

Teaching Visualization Skills

Visualization—seeing the words of a text as mental images in the mind—is a significant factor setting apart proficient readers from low-achieving ones. Studies have shown that the ability to generate vivid images while reading strongly correlates with a person's comprehension of text. However, research has also revealed that *20 percent of all children do not visualize or experience sensory images when reading.* These children are automatically handicapped in their ability to comprehend text, and they are usually the students who avoid and dislike reading because they never connect to text in a personal, meaningful way.

Introduction (cont.)

Active visualization can completely engross a reader in text. You have experienced this when you just could not put a book down, and you stayed up all night just to finish it. Skillful readers automatically weave their own memories into text as they read to make personalized, lifelike images. In fact, every person develops a unique interpretation of any text. This personalized reading experience explains why most people prefer a book to its movie.

Visualization is not static; unlike photographs, these are "movies in the mind." Mental images must constantly be modified to incorporate new information as it is disclosed by the text. Therefore, your students must learn how to revise their images if they encounter information that requires them to do so.

Sensory imaging—employing any of the other senses besides sight—is closely related to visual imaging. It too has been shown to be crucial to the construction of meaning during reading. This is because the more senses that are employed in a task, the more neural pathways are built, resulting in more avenues to access information. You have experienced sensory imaging when you could almost smell the smoke of the forest fire, taste the sizzling bacon, or laughed along with a character as you read. Sensory imaging connects the reader personally and intimately to the text and breathes life into words.

Since visualization is a challenging skill for one out of every five students to develop, begin with simple *fictional* passages to scaffold their attempts and promote success. After your students have experienced success with visualization and sensory imaging in literature, they are ready to employ these techniques in nonfiction text.

Visualization has a special significance in nonfiction text. The technical presentation of ideas in nonfiction text coupled with new terms and concepts often overwhelm and discourage students.

Using visualization can help them to move beyond these barriers. As an added benefit, people who create mental images display better long-term retention of factual material.

Clearly there are important reasons to teach visualization and sensory imaging skills to your students. But perhaps the most compelling reason is this: visualizing demands active involvement, turning passive students into *active* constructors of meaning.

Doing Think-Alouds

It is essential for you to introduce visualization by doing think-alouds to describe your own visualization of text. To do this, read aloud the first one or two lines of a passage and describe what images come to your mind. Be sure to include *details that were not stated in the text,* such as the house has two stories and green shutters. Then read the next two lines and explain how you add to or otherwise modify your image based on the new information provided by the text.

When you are doing a think-aloud for your class, be sure to do the following:

- Explain how your images help you to better understand the passage.
- Describe details, being sure to include some from your own schema.
- Mention the use of your senses—the more the better.
- Describe your revision of the images as you read further and encounter new information.

Introduction *(cont.)*

Teaching Summarizing and Paraphrasing

Summarizing informational text is a crucial skill for students to master. It is also one of the most challenging. Summarizing means pulling out *only* the essential elements of a passage—just the main idea and supporting details. Research has shown that having students put information into their own words causes it to be processed more thoroughly. Thus, paraphrasing increases both understanding and long-term retention of material. Information can be summarized through such diverse activities as speaking, writing, drawing, or creating a project.

The basic steps of summarizing are as follows:

- Look for the paragraph's main idea sentence; if there is none, create one.
- Find the supporting details, being certain to group all related terms or ideas.
- Record information that is repeated or restated only once.
- Put the summary together into an organized format.

Scaffolding is of critical importance. Your students will need a lot of modeling, guided practice, and small group or partner practice before attempting to summarize independently. All strategies should be done as a whole group and then with a partner several times before letting the students do it on their own. Encourage the greatest transfer of knowledge by modeling each strategy's use in multiple content areas.

Teaching Vocabulary

In the early years, students may start seeing words in print that they may have never seen before in either print or oral language. As a result, these students need direct instruction in vocabulary to make real progress toward becoming readers who can independently access expository text. Teaching the vocabulary that occurs in a text significantly improves comprehension. Since students encounter vocabulary terms in science, social studies, math, and language arts, strategies for decoding and understanding new words must be taught throughout the day.

Students' vocabularies develop following this progression: listening, speaking, reading, and writing. This means that a child understands a word when it is spoken to him long before he uses it in his own speaking. The child will also understand the word when he reads it before he will attempt to use it in his own writing. Each time a child comes across the same word, his or her understanding of that word deepens. Research has shown that vocabulary instruction has the most positive effect on reading comprehension when students encounter the words multiple times. That is why the best vocabulary instruction requires students to use new words in writing and speaking as well as in reading.

Teaching vocabulary can be both effective and fun, especially if you engage the students' multiple modalities (listening, speaking, reading, and writing). In addition, instruction that uses all four modalities is most apt to reach every learner.

The more experience a child has with language, the stronger his or her vocabulary base. Therefore, the majority of vocabulary activities should be done as whole-group or small-group instruction. In this way children with a limited vocabulary can learn from their peers' knowledge base and will find vocabulary activities less frustrating. Remember, too, that a picture is worth a thousand words. Whenever possible provide a picture of a new vocabulary word.

Introduction *(cont.)*

Selecting Vocabulary Words to Study

Many teachers feel overwhelmed when teaching vocabulary because they realize that it is impossible to thoroughly cover all students' unknown words. Do not attempt to study every unknown word. Instead, choose the words from each selection wisely. Following these guidelines will result in an educationally sound vocabulary list:

- First choose words that are critical to the article's meaning.
- Then choose conceptually difficult words.
- Finally choose words with the greatest utility value—those that you anticipate the children will see more often (*e.g.*, choose *anxious* rather than *appalled*).

These suggestions are given for teaching nonfiction material in general. *Do not select and preteach vocabulary from these practice passages.* You want to simulate real test conditions in which the children would have no prior knowledge of any of the material in any of the passages.

Elements of Effective Vocabulary Instruction

Vocabulary instruction is only effective if children permanently add the concepts to their knowledge base. Research has shown that the most effective vocabulary program includes contextual, structural, and classification strategies. You can do this by making certain that your vocabulary instruction includes the following elements:

- using context clues
- knowing the meaning of affixes (prefixes, suffixes) and roots
- introducing new words as synonyms and antonyms of known words

Using Context Clues

Learning vocabulary in context is important for two reasons. First, it makes children become active in determining word meanings, and second, it transfers into their lives by offering them a way to figure out unknown words in their independent reading. If you teach your students how to use context clues, you may eventually be able to omit preteaching any vocabulary that is defined in context (so long as the text is written at your students' independent level).

There are five basic kinds of context clues.

1. **Definition:** The easiest case is when the definition is given elsewhere in the sentence or paragraph.

   example: The ragged, *tattered* dress hung from her shoulders.

2. **Synonym:** Another simple case is when a synonym or synonymous phrase is immediately used.

   example: Although she was fat, her *obesity* never bothered her until she went to middle school.

3. **Contrast:** The meaning may be implied through contrast to a known word or concept. Be alert to these words that signal contrast: although, but, however, even though.

   example: Although Adesha had always been *prompt*, today he was 20 minutes late.

Introduction *(cont.)*

4. **Summary:** Another form is summary, which sums up a list of attributes.

   example: Tundra, desert, grassland, and rain forest are four of the Earth's *biomes*.

5. **Mood:** Sometimes the meaning can be grasped from the mood of the larger context in which it appears. The most difficult situation is when the meaning must be inferred with few other clues.

   example: Her *shrill* voice was actually making my ears hurt.

Your general approach to building vocabulary should include the following:

Brainstorming: Students brainstorm a list of words associated with a familiar word, sharing everyone's knowledge and discussing unfamiliar words thoroughly.

Semantic mapping: Students sort the brainstormed words into categories, often creating a visual organization tool—such as a graphic organizer or word web—to depict the relationships.

Feature analysis: You provide key features and a list of terms in a chart, such as a semantic matrix or Venn diagram. Have students identify the similarities and differences between the items.

Synonyms and antonyms: Introducing both synonyms and antonyms for the terms you study provides a structure for meaning and substantially increases your students' vocabulary rapidly.

Analogies: Analogies are similar to synonyms but require higher-level thinking. The goal is to help students identify the relationship between words. Analogies appear on standardized tests in the upper elementary grades.

example: Bark is to tree as skin is to <u>human</u>.

Word affixes: Studying common prefixes and suffixes will help students deduce new words, especially in context. Teach students to ask, "Does this look like any other word I know? Can I find any word parts I know? Can I figure out the meaning based on its context?"

Introduction *(cont.)*

Important Affixes for Primary Grades

Prefix	Meaning	Example	Suffix	Meaning	Example
un	not	unusual	**-s or -es**	more than one	cars; tomatoes
re	again	redo	**-ed**	did an action	moved
in, im	not	impassable	**-ing**	doing an action	buying
dis	opposite	disassemble	**-ly**	like, very	usually
non	not	nonathletic	**-er**	a person who	farmer
over	too much	overcook	**-ful**	full of	respectful
mis	bad	misrepresent	**-or**	a person who	creator
pre	before	prearrange	**-less**	without	harmless
de	opposite	decompose	**-er**	more	calmer
under	less	underachieve	**-est**	most	happiest

Directions: Read the story.

The Sixth Great Lake

The five Great Lakes are very big. How big? They can be seen from space! And Lake Superior is the second biggest lake in the world. These lakes hold one-fifth of all the fresh water in the world. Fresh water is not salty like sea water. People can drink fresh water.

The five Great Lakes are linked. A ship can move from one to the other. A ship can go all the way from Lake Superior to Lake Ontario. Many ships move from lake to lake, bringing goods to people.

The U.S. government gives scientists money to study the Great Lakes. In 1998, President Clinton signed a law. It made Lake Champlain a Great Lake. Now scientists would get money to study that lake, too. But many people did not like the law. They thought that Lake Champlain should not be called a Great Lake. After all, Lake Ontario is the smallest Great Lake. And it is 15 times bigger than Lake Champlain! So Lake Champlain was a Great Lake for just 18 days. Then the law was changed. But there is still a lot to learn about Lake Champlain. So the scientists will still get money to study the lake.

The Sixth Great Lake (cont.)

Directions: Answer these questions. You may look at the story.

1. What is this passage about?

    a. salt water

    b. the Great Lakes

    c. Lake Superior

2. Is Lake Champlain a Great Lake now?

    a. No, it is still waiting for a law to make it a Great Lake.

    b. No, it has never been a Great Lake.

    c. No, it has not been a Great Lake since 1998.

3. Why was the law changed?

    _____

    _____

    _____

4. Do you think that the scientists were glad when Lake Champlain was named a Great Lake?

    _____

    _____

    _____

5. What do you think the scientists probably study about the Great Lakes?

    _____

    _____

    _____

6. What can people who live near the Great Lakes do with all the fresh water they have?

    _____

    _____

    _____

7. Why is it important for the Great Lakes to be studied? Explain.

    _____

    _____

The Sixth Great Lake *(cont.)*

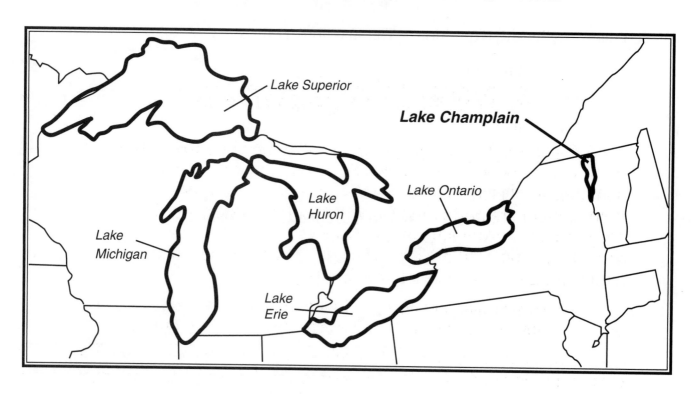

Look at the map. Do you think that Lake Champlain should be called a Great Lake? Explain.

_____

_____

_____

_____

_____

_____

_____

Directions: Read the story.

A New Dinosaur Pair

A scientist was digging in Utah. Then he got a big surprise. He found the bones of two new kinds of dinosaurs. No one knew about these dinosaurs. No one had ever seen such bones before. Both of them are part of the same group. The group is called ankylosaurs (*an*-kuh-luh-sores). Scientists knew that this group of animals was here 70 million years ago. But these bones are 95 million years old.

These animals had horns. They had hard, thick plates on their bodies. They could grow to be over 30 feet long. They ate plants.

One is an ankylosaurid (*an*-kuh-luh-sore-id). It had a heavy club at the end of its long tail. It used this club to stay safe. When it swung its tail, it could fight off big animals.

The other is a nodosaurid (*no*-duh-sore-id). It had big spikes on its shoulders. If another animal wanted to eat it, the dinosaur could ram it with these spikes. Ouch!

A New Dinosaur Pair *(cont.)*

Directions: Answer these questions. You may look at the story.

1. What did the scientist dig up in Utah?

    a. an old village

    b. a graveyard

    c. new kinds of dinosaur bones

2. What could the nodosaurid use to fight off bigger animals?

    a. horns and a club on its tail

    b. horns and spikes

    c. horns and claws

3. What did the scientist's find prove?

    _____

    _____

    _____

4. Why did the ankylosaurs have thick, heavy plates on their bodies?

    _____

    _____

    _____

5. What do you think this article shows about finding dinosaurs?

    _____

    _____

    _____

6. How did the nodosaurid differ from the ankylosaurid?

    _____

    _____

    _____

7. If you were a predator, which of these ankylosaurs would you rather try to eat? Explain.

    _____

    _____

    _____

A New Dinosaur Pair *(cont.)*

Read this newspaper advertisement. Answer the question.

Come to the New Exhibit

WHEN DINOSAURS WALKED THE EARTH

March 12—October 12

at the American Science Center
3542 Hudson Avenue

See complete skeletons of:

- Ankylosaurid
- Stegosaurus
- Dimetrodon
- Triceratops

Videos, speakers, and hands-on activities . . . fun for everyone!

What do you think you could learn from this exhibit? Explain.

_____

_____

_____

_____

Rings Around Jupiter

Jupiter is a big ball of liquid. Gases swirl around it. It does not have a solid surface. But Jupiter is the king of the planets. It is very big. Its Great Red Spot is two times bigger than our Earth. Jupiter is so big that all of the other planets could fit inside of it!

A few years ago scientists saw new pictures of Jupiter. These pictures were taken in space. The scientists already knew that Jupiter has rings. They wanted to know how it got the rings. The new pictures helped them to see how the rings were formed. The rings are made of moondust.

Where does the moondust come from? It comes from one of Jupiter's 16 moons. Jupiter has strong gravity. Gravity is what holds things down on the ground. Jupiter's gravity pulls on space rocks. It pulls them closer and closer. Some of these rocks hit the moons around Jupiter. The crash makes a big dust cloud. This cloud starts to circle the planet. Then we see it as one of the many rings around Jupiter.

Rings Around Jupiter *(cont.)*

Directions: Answer these questions. You may look at the story.

1. How many moons does Jupiter have?

    a. 6

    b. 16

    c. No one knows.

2. What does Jupiter's gravity do to rocks out in space?

    a. It pulls them closer.

    b. It pushes them away.

    c. It turns them into moons.

3. What happens after space rocks hit Jupiter's moons and moondust forms?

    _____

    _____

    _____

4. What is an important feature of Jupiter?

    _____

    _____

    _____

5. What did the writer do to help you understand Jupiter's size?

    _____

    _____

    _____

6. What do we know for sure about Jupiter?

    _____

    _____

    _____

7. If you could, would you like to travel to Jupiter someday? Explain.

    _____

    _____

    _____

Rings Around Jupiter *(cont.)*

Jupiter has more than a dozen moons, but Earth has only one moon. Earth's moon reflects the sun's light to us. The moon seems to change shape. But it really does not. The Earth throws its shadow on the moon. So, the amount of the moon we see is based on how much of it is in shadow. Thus the moon goes through "phases." It takes about one month to complete one cycle. Here is one cycle of the moon:

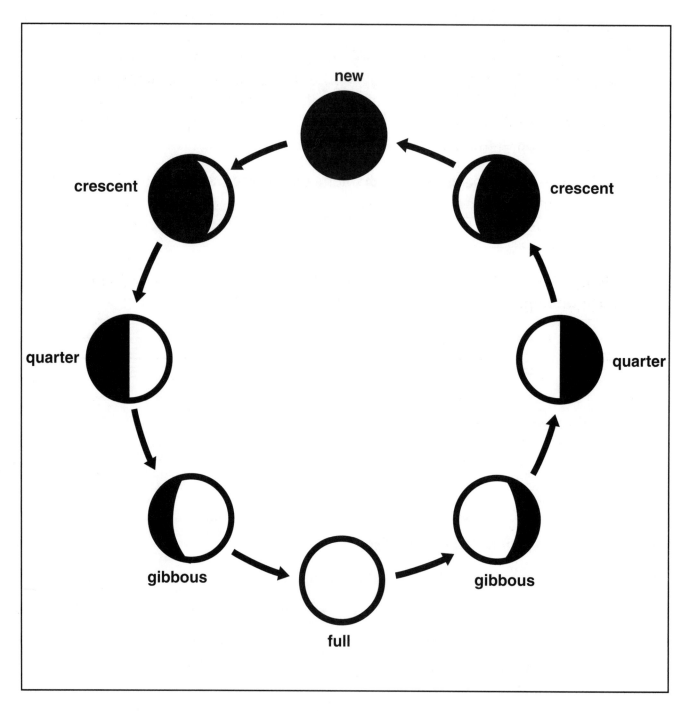

On the back of this paper, explain the difference between a new moon and a full moon.

A Lucky Brake

Kids can be heroes. Larry Champagne is only 10. But he is a hero. He saved a whole school bus full of kids. The kids were on their way to school. Their bus driver passed out in his seat. No one was driving the bus! The bus started to bang into fences along the side of the road. Kids screamed. They were all afraid. Then Larry ran to the front and stopped the bus. How did he do it? He pushed hard on the brake. No one was hurt. Larry had saved the day!

Larry knows about brakes because he helps his grandfather work on his truck. Larry said he pushed the brake because, "My grandmother always tells me to do what's right."

Larry's story made news all over the country. He was on TV. His school gave him a medal. But the kids on that bus already knew that he was a real hero.

A Lucky Brake *(cont.)*

Directions: Answer these questions. You may look at the story.

1. What did Larry Champagne do?

    a. He stopped a runaway bus.

    b. He fixed a truck.

    c. He saved a kitten.

2. How did Larry know where the brake was?

    a. He was a school bus driver.

    b. His grandfather had shown him the brakes on a truck.

    c. He had taken driving lessons.

3. What probably would have happened if Larry had not stopped the bus?

    _____

    _____

    _____

4. Why do you think the author wrote this story?

    _____

    _____

    _____

5. Why do you think Larry received a medal?

    _____

    _____

    _____

6. If Larry saw a fire, what do you think he would do?

    _____

    _____

    _____

7. Do you think that Larry Champagne is a hero? Explain.

    _____

    _____

    _____

A Lucky Brake (cont.)

Read this newspaper article. Answer the question.

The California Chronicle

August 25, 1995

CALIFORNIA, API—The Gallegos family is very glad that Joe Terry lives on R Street in Merced. Last night this brave 15-year-old saved the two Gallegos tots in a daring rescue on the tracks.

Josh Gallegos, 3, and his sister, Jenny, 1, had left their yard. They went to play on the railroad tracks. Their mother did not know where they were.

As the 8:25 train came racing at them at 60 miles an hour, Jenny sat on a rail. Josh stood between the rails. He was picking up rocks.

Joe Terry was on his front porch. He looked across the road. He saw the tiny children on the tracks. He heard the train coming. Joe started to run. He ran across four lanes of traffic. He was almost hit. But he did not slow down.

When he reached the children, Joe shoved Josh out of the way and grabbed Jenny. Holding her, he jumped. The train was so close that it knocked his baseball cap off his head. The children's mother says she will never stop being thankful that Joe got there in time.

Governor Wilson says that Joe Terry will be given the Carnegie Medal for Bravery.

Joe Terry got the Carnegie Medal for Bravery. Do you think Larry Champagne should be given it, too? Explain.

_____

_____

_____

_____

Racing a Tornado!

The day started out beautiful. Maria and I went for a long bike ride. Little did we know we would end up racing a tornado!

We rode far away from home. Then the temperature suddenly dropped. The sky turned a dark greenish color. A very strong wind started to blow. A blue car pulled up beside us. "Get in!" the driver said. It was my aunt. She looked very scared. We got in the car.

It's a good thing we did. Pieces of hail the size of golf balls hit the car. Maria looked over her shoulder and screamed, "Tornado!" The tornado was so close I could see doors and trees spinning around in it! My aunt was going as fast as she could. But she knew that she couldn't outrun the tornado. She saw a bridge. She stopped the car. We all ran to get under the bridge. We laid flat, pressed up against the wall of the bridge. Then the tornado hit the bridge. It sounded like a train. It quickly passed by. The bridge held! We were safe.

What a story I would have to tell at school!

Racing a Tornado! *(cont.)*

Directions: Answer these questions. You may look at the story.

1. What were the girls doing when the storm began?

    a. walking along the road

    b. biking along the road

    c. sitting by the road

2. A tornado is a kind of . . .

    a. windstorm

    b. snowstorm

    c. sandstorm

3. Why did the driver look scared?

    _____

    _____

    _____

4. What would have happened if the girls had not gotten into the car?

    _____

    _____

    _____

5. Why did the writer tell us about the size of the hail?

    _____

    _____

    _____

6. Which is the best place to be during a tornado?

    _____

    _____

    _____

7. How would you have felt if you were under the bridge with Maria? Explain.

    _____

    _____

    _____

Racing a Tornado! _(cont.)_

Read this safety brochure. Answer the question.

Tornado Safety Tips

1. Tornadoes often happen in the spring or summer. If you are in a place that has tornadoes, always keep a radio turned on. That way you will hear any warnings.

2. When you hear a warning, _take shelter_! Bring only people and pets. Do not spend time trying to save things.

3. A good place to be is **under the basement stairs**. An **underground storm shelter** is the best place to be.

4. If you do not have a basement or a storm shelter, go to the **first floor** of your home. Crawl under a table along an **inside wall**. An inside wall does not touch the outside of the house. Crouch down. Cover your head with your hands.

5. In any other building, get to an **inside hall** on the **ground floor**. Crouch down. Cover your head with your hands.

6. If you are caught outside, lie face down in a **ditch**.

Look at the words in **dark print**. Why do you think these places are the safest during a tornado? Explain. _____

_____

_____

Hooked on Harry

Do you feel the magic spell in the air? The spell comes from J. K. Rowling. Her pen is a magic wand. She writes the Harry Potter books. Although they are pretty long, these books are very popular. They are being made into movies.

When Harry Potter finds out that he is a boy wizard, he goes to Hogwarts School of Witchcraft and Wizardry. He has lots of adventures there. There will be one book for each of the seven years that Harry is in the school.

J. K. Rowling says, "I don't know where Harry came from. He just strolled into my head!" Kids are sure glad that he did. How will it all end? Rowling says the last word of the last book is "scar."

Hooked on Harry *(cont.)*

Directions: Answer these questions. You may look at the story.

1. Who writes the Harry Potter books?

    a. J. K. Potter

    b. J. K. Hogwarts

    c. J. K. Rowling

2. How many books will be in the Harry Potter series?

    a. 5

    b. 7

    c. 8

3. What is taught at Hogwarts?

_____

_____

_____

4. Why are the books being made into movies?

_____

_____

_____

5. How is Harry Potter different from other boys?

_____

_____

_____

6. Why do you think the Harry Potter books are so popular?

_____

_____

_____

7. Would you like to read the Harry Potter books? Explain.

_____

_____

_____

Hooked on Harry (cont.)

Suppose J. K. Rowling decided to write a book about a girl wizard, Sara Grayfield. Look at the front cover of the first book. What kinds of adventures do you think Sara has?

_____

_____

_____

_____

Directions: Read the story.

Aliens in Lake Victoria

There are aliens in Lake Victoria in Africa! No, they are not from outer space. These aliens are plants. They have purple flowers. The plants are water hyacinths (hi-uh-sinths). They come from South America. Now they are filling up the biggest lake in Africa. No one knows how the plants got there.

The plants grow close together. They form a blanket. They completely cover the water. This traps fishing boats. The people who live near the lake cannot go fishing. And they need to fish to get food and money.

Some scientists are using tiny beetles to fight back. The beetles eat the plants. Other people use a big machine. They call it the Swamp Devil. It cuts up the plants. But some people worry that it may kill too many of the plants. Some of the fish in the lake eat the water hyacinths.

Aliens in Lake Victoria *(cont.)*

Directions: Answer these questions. You may look at the story.

1. What is the name of the machine?

   a. Swamp Devil

   b. Hyacinth Cutter

   c. Beetle

2. Why are water hyacinths called aliens in the article?

   a. because they come from a place far away from Lake Victoria

   b. because they are from outer space

   c. because they are against the law

3. Why are the people who fish upset about the plants?

   _____

   _____

   _____

4. How many lakes in Africa are smaller than Lake Victoria?

   _____

   _____

   _____

5. Why was the Swamp Devil used?

   _____

   _____

   _____

6. How do most people feel about the water hyacinths?

   _____

   _____

   _____

7. Should the Swamp Devil or the beetles be used on the water hyacinths? Explain.

   _____

   _____

   _____

Aliens in Lake Victoria *(cont.)*

Read this magazine article. Answer the question.

Today's Environment   *December 2002*

Zebra Mussels Trouble

A small animal came to the Great Lakes in 1986. It was the zebra mussel. A ship probably carried zebra mussels into one of the lakes. The ship had come from the ocean. The zebra mussels had no predators in the Great Lakes. They grew and grew. They spread from lake to lake. Soon there were too many zebra mussels.

Zebra mussels eat algae. This makes the water much clearer. But it also makes the water more acidic. And they have eaten so much algae that most other animals that eat algae have died.

Now people are worried about the mussels. They don't like them. They don't like how they have changed the lake. But they are hard to get rid of. They must be kept from spreading. So when a boat is taken out of the water, its bottom is scraped.

page 176

How are zebra mussels in the Great Lakes like the water hyacinths in Lake Victoria?

_____

_____

_____

_____

Directions: Read the story.

People Should Not Capture Whales

Have you ever seen a whale at a sea park? It is fun to see these big wet animals. But people should not keep whales in water parks. They should be in the ocean. Whales should swim all over the ocean.

In 1997 a baby gray whale washed up on a beach. She was hungry and sick. Workers at Sea World in San Diego saved her. They gave her a drink that was like the milk of a mother whale. The baby whale, named J.J., grew bigger. In fact, she gained about two pounds every hour! At last she was 29 feet long. She weighed more than 17,000 pounds.

The Sea World workers put J.J. back into the ocean. They knew that she should not be kept in a water park. And they knew that other whales would teach her to get food.

People Should Not Capture Whales *(cont.)*

Directions: Answer these questions. You may look at the story.

1. How fast did J.J. grow?
    a. one pound every hour
    b. two pounds every hour
    c. three pounds every hour

2. What did the workers feed J.J.?
    a. her mother's milk
    b. something like whale's milk
    c. fish

3. What probably would have happened to J.J. if the Sea World workers had not found her?

    _____

    _____

    _____

4. If another baby whale washes up, what do you think the Sea World workers will do?

    _____

    _____

    _____

5. How do you think the Sea World workers felt about returning J.J. to the ocean?

    _____

    _____

    _____

6. Will J.J. have a hard time living in the ocean?

    _____

    _____

    _____

7. Do you think that whales should be kept in water parks? Explain.

    _____

    _____

    _____

People Should Not Capture Whales *(cont.)*

Look at the photo. Why do you think that people like to have whales at water parks? Explain.

_____

_____

_____

The Big Chill

The people who live in Alaska are used to the cold. But in February 1999, even they said that it was very cold. How cold was it? The temperature dropped to –77°F. Strong winds made it feel like –107°F! It was so cold that boiling water thrown into the air instantly turned into ice!

Snow turns powdery and dry when it's so cold. Walking on it makes a weird, squeaky noise. It sounds like rubbing Styrofoam. People can't talk because their lips are so numb. It may hurt to breathe such cold air. But that's not the worst that can happen.

Deep cold causes problems. Fuel gets thicker. It can't flow through an engine. So things like planes and buses can't move. Car and bus tires go flat. Things made of wood, plastic, and metal snap. Trees crack and fall over. Pipes burst when the water inside of them freezes. It's hard to make gas stoves work. After it reaches –20°F, the teachers will not let the kids go out for recess.

The Big Chill (cont.)

Directions: Answer these questions. You may look at the story.

1. What is the lowest temperature recorded in February 1999, in Alaska?

    a. –20°F

    b. –77°F

    c. –107°F

2. What would happen to hot coffee in such cold?

    a. It would quickly change into ice.

    b. It would keep boiling.

    c. It would turn into powdery snow.

3. Which probably kept working during the Big Chill?

    a. snowmobiles

    b. electric heaters

    c. helicopters

4. Why does the writer mention Styrofoam?

    _____

    _____

    _____

5. Why do you think that the teachers keep the kids inside when it gets to –20°F?

    _____

    _____

    _____

6. What was dangerous to do during the Big Chill?

    _____

    _____

    _____

7. Which kind of weather do you like better, really cold or really hot? Explain.

    _____

    _____

    _____

The Big Chill *(cont.)*

Use this graph to answer the questions below.

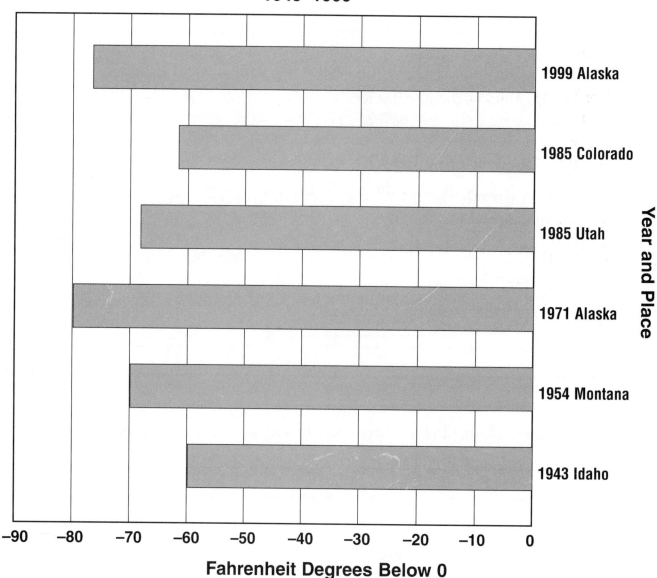

Coldest Temperatures in USA
1943–1999

1999 Alaska

1985 Colorado

1985 Utah

1971 Alaska

1954 Montana

1943 Idaho

Year and Place

−90 −80 −70 −60 −50 −40 −30 −20 −10 0

Fahrenheit Degrees Below 0

Before the Big Chill in 1999, had it ever before been so cold in the USA? If yes, where?

_____

Why do you think that the two coldest temperatures are in the same state?

_____

_____

A Dream Come True

When Hannah Kristan was small, she did not like school recess. She never got to do anything. She had to just sit there. That's because Hannah was born with a problem. The problem kept the bones in her back from growing the right way. So, she can't do many of the things that most kids can do. She uses a wheelchair. But kids in wheelchairs can't play with their friends on school playgrounds. They can't use the swings. They can't use the slides.

Then Hannah heard about special playgrounds for disabled kids. She helped to raise money for one in her town. This new playground has a high-back swing that helps her to sit up. Now she can swing! Hannah really enjoys the new playground.

Hannah says, "Disabled people are just like anybody else. We want to be able to play with our friends."

A Dream Come True (cont.)

Directions: Answer these questions. You may look at the story.

1. Why didn't Hannah like recess?
   a. She had no friends.
   b. She didn't like playgrounds.
   c. She had nothing to do.

2. What did Hannah do to get a playground she could use?
   a. She studied hard.
   b. She got the law changed.
   c. She helped raise money.

3. Why did Hannah want a special playground?

   _____

   _____

   _____

4. Why can't a kid in a wheelchair use a regular playground?

   _____

   _____

   _____

5. How is Hannah like every other kid?

   _____

   _____

   _____

6. Can disabled people have fun?

   _____

   _____

   _____

7. What do you think would be the hardest thing about being in a wheelchair? Explain.

   _____

   _____

   _____

A Dream Come True (cont.)

Here is information from a Web site. Read it and answer the question.

The Paralympics

The Paralympics are very much like the Olympics. But they are for people with disabilities. Some of the Paralympians are blind. Some may not be able to move their legs. Many do not have an arm or a leg. They play against others who have the same kinds of problems.

The Paralympics always take place right after the Olympic Games or the Olympic Winter Games. They are held in the same place. The top three athletes in each sport get medals. More than 4,000 people took part in the 2000 Paralympics.

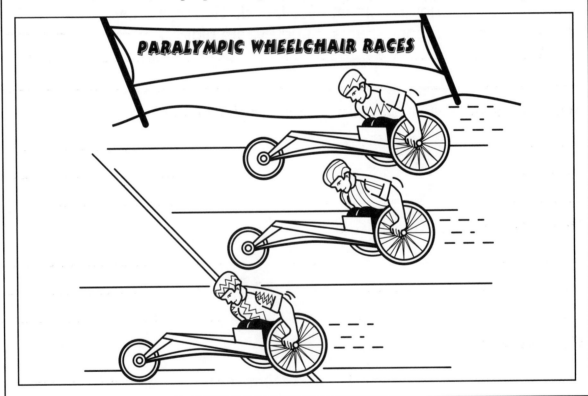

Why are the Paralympics important to someone like Hannah Kristan? Explain.

_____

_____

_____

_____

The Sound of Old Music

Scientists were digging in China. There they found parts of old homes and clay pots. They also found 36 tubes. Each tube had five to seven holes. They figured out that these tubes were flutes. The flutes were made from bird bones about 9,000 years ago.

One of the flutes had no cracks. It could still make music! So the scientists tried to play it. "It makes a pleasant sound," one scientist said. That flute may be the oldest musical instrument ever played. But it is not the oldest ever found. Scientists have found a flute made from a bone that is 33,000 years old!

The Sound of Old Music *(cont.)*

Directions: Answer these questions. You may look at the story.

1. Where were the scientists digging?

    a. in China

    b. in South America

    c. in Africa

2. Why did the tubes have holes?

    a. to look nice

    b. so they would not hold water

    c. to make different sounds

3. What does this passage tell us about how long music has been around?

    _____

    _____

    _____

4. Why do you think scientists like to dig up things that people used so long ago?

    _____

    _____

    _____

5. What did the scientists' find tell them about the Chinese people of long ago?

    _____

    _____

    _____

6. Why do you think scientists were excited about what they found?

    _____

    _____

    _____

7. Why do you think people played flutes so long ago? Explain.

    _____

    _____

    _____

The Sound of Old Music (cont.)

Look at this wall mosaic.

What other instruments did ancient people play beside flutes?

_____

_____

_____

_____

Treasures in the Sand

A man was riding his donkey. They were on a road in Egypt. Egypt is in North Africa. Then the donkey fell. Its leg went into a hole. The man looked down in the hole. He saw lots of mummies! They were stacked on top of each other. He told others what he had seen.

So in 1999, mummy experts went there to dig. They found bracelets and charms. They found pots and coins. They found walls with painted pictures. Some of the walls have special symbols. The symbols were an old form of writing.

They found some mummies covered in gold. The mummies had been there for about 2,000 years. So far the team has uncovered more than 100 mummies. But there may be up to 10,000 mummies buried there.

Treasures in the Sand *(cont.)*

Directions: Answer these questions. You may look at the story.

1. How did the mummies first get found?

    a. Mummy experts dug them up.

    b. A donkey fell in a hole.

    c. A storm blew the sand off of them.

2. What is a mummy?

    a. A dead body prepared in a special way.

    b. A woman who has a child.

    c. An expert on very old things.

3. What did the experts find at the dig?

    _____

    _____

    _____

4. What does the author mean by the word *treasures* in the title?

    _____

    _____

    _____

5. Why do you think the symbols were probably on the walls?

    _____

    _____

    _____

6. Why do you think some of the mummies were covered in gold?

    _____

    _____

    _____

7. Would you like to search for mummies? Explain.

    _____

    _____

    _____

Treasures in the Sand *(cont.)*

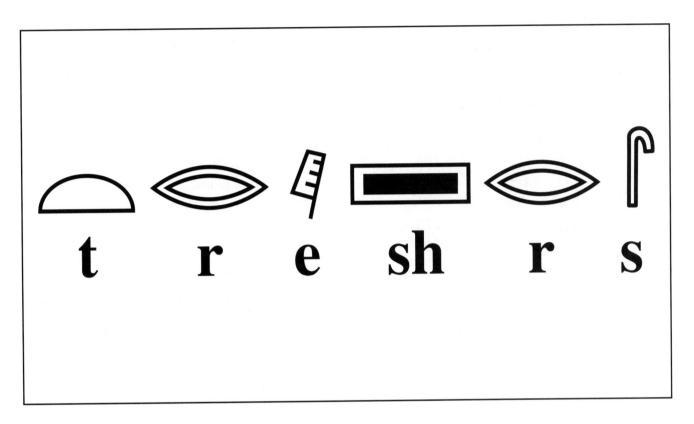

Here is an example of the writing on the walls where the mummies were found.
It says, "treasures."

Do you think that it is easier to write with letters or symbols? Explain.

_____

_____

_____

_____

Directions: Read the story.

Secrets of the Giant Squid

It lies in a big plastic case in the American Museum of Natural History. Many people come to see it. They can't believe their eyes.

What is it? It's a dead giant squid. This male squid was found near New Zealand. It weighs 200 pounds. It is 25 feet long. A female would be twice as long! It has eyes the size of volleyballs. It has eight arms and two tentacles. Each of the giant squid's arms has rows of tiny, sharp teeth.

Not much is known about the giant squid. Few have been found. No one has ever seen a giant squid alive. Some scientists think that they can get to be 60 feet long and weigh over a ton! But no one knows where they live. No one knows how many there are. That's because giant squid are found in deep sea waters—as deep as 3,000 feet!

Secrets of the Giant Squid *(cont.)*

Directions: Answer these questions. You may look at the story.

1. Where is this giant squid kept?

   a. at the American Museum

   b. at the New York Museum of Natural History

   c. at the American Museum of Natural History

2. Where was this giant squid discovered?

   a. near New York City

   b. near New Zealand

   c. near New Guinea

3. If it were the same age as the dead one, how long would a female giant squid probably be?

   _____

   _____

   _____

4. Why is so little known about giant squid?

   _____

   _____

   _____

5. What other sea creature is similar to a giant squid?

   _____

   _____

   _____

6. Are you likely to be in danger of a giant squid attack at the beach?

   _____

   _____

   _____

7. Would you rather see a dead or a living giant squid? Explain.

   _____

   _____

Secrets of the Giant Squid *(cont.)*

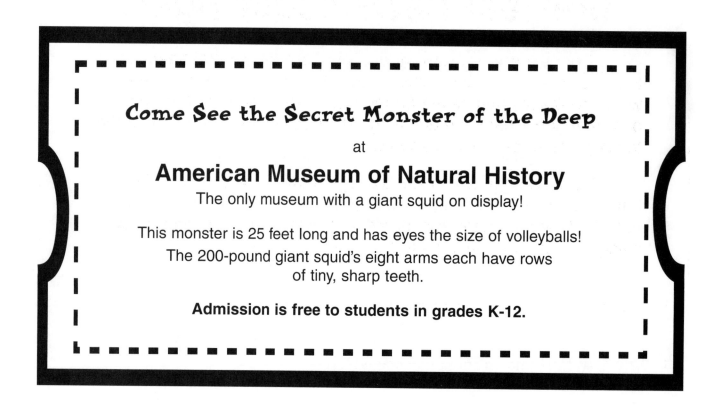

Come See the Secret Monster of the Deep

at

American Museum of Natural History

The only museum with a giant squid on display!

This monster is 25 feet long and has eyes the size of volleyballs!
The 200-pound giant squid's eight arms each have rows
of tiny, sharp teeth.

Admission is free to students in grades K-12.

Look at the ticket. What would it cost you to go to see the giant squid? Why do you think the museum set that price?

_____

_____

_____

_____

Directions: Read the story.

Gr-r-reat News About Tigers

Tiger experts were worried. Five different kinds of tigers used to live all over Asia. But hunters had killed many of them. There were few grassy homes left for the tigers. And the deer and wild boar that tigers eat were almost gone. Tiger experts were afraid that the big striped cats would soon disappear, too.

But now at least two kinds of tigers are coming back. They have land to live on. They have prey to catch. So they have food to eat. And they are safe from hunters. "Tigers are still in danger of dying out. But we feel hopeful," said one tiger expert.

Gr-r-reat News About Tigers *(cont.)*

Directions: Answer these questions. You may look at the story.

1. How many different types of tigers used to live in Asia?

    a. three

    b. four

    c. five

2. Why did tiger experts worry?

    a. The tigers were running out of land and food.

    b. The tigers were not having enough cubs.

    c. The tigers were getting sick easily.

3. How do wild boars relate to tigers?

    _____

    _____

    _____

4. What things does a tiger need in order to survive?

    _____

    _____

    _____

5. Why do you think that some tigers are now safe from hunters?

    _____

    _____

    _____

6. If all of the tigers were gone, what might happen to the deer and wild boar?

    _____

    _____

    _____

7. Why do you think the deer and the wild boar were disappearing? Explain.

    _____

    _____

    _____

Read this poem. Answer the question.

Tigers

Today great striped cats still run free,

but with so few left it makes me worry.

Hunters killed too much of their prey

and hurt the tigers in the same way.

With their homes disappearing

and less food to eat,

many tigers died due to lack of meat.

Should we help the tigers?

Of course we should!

More tigers will live if we just would.

—Anonymous

How would the writer of this poem feel about a law to keep tigers from being hunted?
Explain.

_____

_____

_____

_____

Directions: Read the story.

Around the World in 20 Days

Many people wanted to be the first to fly around the world in a hot air balloon. A lot of people tried, but they could not do it. Then Bertrand Piccard and Brian Jones did it. In 1999, they went all the way around the world in their hot air balloon.

On March 1, the men took off from Switzerland. Then they flew their balloon more than 29,000 miles. They landed in Egypt on March 21. Their trip had taken 20 days. It had been hard for them. The men got very tired. They got very cold. But in the end they were very happy. They had made history. They were the first people to go around the world in a hot air balloon!

Around the World in 20 Days *(cont.)*

Directions: Answer these questions. You may look at the story.

1. What are Bertrand Piccard and Brian Jones famous for doing?

    a. They flew a balloon from Egypt to Switzerland.

    b. They stayed in a hot air balloon for 20 days.

    c. They flew all the way around the world in a hot air balloon.

2. How long did the trip take?

    a. less than a month

    b. a month

    c. more than a month

3. What real dangers did the men face on their trip?

    _____

    _____

    _____

4. Why do you think the men got so cold on their trip?

    _____

    _____

    _____

5. Why do you think so many other people who tried failed?

    _____

    _____

    _____

6. What happens when someone makes history?

    _____

    _____

    _____

7. Visit Mars . . . live on the moon in a space station . . . travel at the speed of light. What would you like to be the first person to do? Explain.

    _____

    _____

    _____

Around the World in 20 Days *(cont.)*

Many people say that they have seen UFOs. UFO stands for Unidentified Flying Object. But most UFOs turn out to be something normal. In fact, some people saw Orbiter 3 and thought that it was a UFO! Look at this graph. Then answer the questions.

For Every 20 UFO Sightings	
planes	✈ ✈ ✈ ✈ ✈ ✈ ✈ ✈
searchlights	🔦 🔦 🔦 🔦 🔦
blimps	⬭ ⬭ ⬭
UFOs	🛸 🛸
balloons	🎈
satellites	🛰

When do you think most UFO sightings happen—during the day or at night?

_____

_____

Why do you think that most UFOs turn out to be planes?

_____

_____

Directions: Read the story.

New Champs Take the Court

In tennis, players hit a little ball over a low net. They use a racquet to hit the ball. Sometimes there are two players. Sometimes there are four players. To win at tennis, you have to be fast. You have to hit the ball hard, but not too hard. It takes a lot of practice to get good at the game.

Now two sisters are U.S. tennis champs. Their names are Serena and Venus Williams. Serena won the U.S. Open. It was a very hard contest. Winning made Serena the "singles" champ. She won almost $1 million!

Then Serena and Venus played together. They played in a "doubles" contest. They played against two other girls. They played hard and won. So the two sisters are the new "doubles" champs!

Both of the girls are very good athletes. Serena has been playing tennis since she was 5. But she says, "Tennis is just a game. It's not your life. We really believe in family."

New Champs Take the Court *(cont.)*

Directions: Answer these questions. You may look at the story.

1. How is tennis played?

    a. by hitting a ball

    b. by rolling a ball

    c. by throwing a ball

2. Who holds two titles?

    a. Serena

    b. Venus

    c. both sisters

3. How did Serena get so good at tennis?

    _____

    _____

    _____

4. Why do you think Serena and Venus Williams tried to win the U.S. Open?

    _____

    _____

    _____

5. What other sport is like tennis?

    _____

    _____

    _____

6. Which words best sum up this passage?

    _____

    _____

    _____

7. What do other sports have in common with tennis? Explain.

    _____

    _____

    _____

New Champs Take the Court *(cont.)*

Read this e-mail message.

Subject: I'm a fan!

Date: December 8, 2002

From: kameela@myhouse.com

To: Serena Williams

Dear Serena,

I have played tennis since I was 8 years old. I want to be just like you. I know that your dad really helped you to become a tennis star. My mom is helping me. She is paying for my lessons. I am getting better all the time.

I was so happy when you won the U.S. Open Singles title. Then when you won the Doubles title with your sister, I knew that you were the best tennis player ever! You are amazing.

I read in a magazine that your favorite instrument was a guitar. Do you know how to play?

I also read that your favorite place to visit is Indian Wells, California. I live about an hour away from there! I would love to meet you sometime.

Your biggest fan,

Kameela Jefferson

Why do you think that Kameela sent this e-mail to Serena?

_____

_____

_____

_____

Hello! Anybody Out There?

What do aliens from outer space look like? Are they short and green? tall and purple? Do they have pink stripes? red spots? Are there really any aliens? Today we may have the tools to find out. So scientists look for signs of life in outer space.

How do they look? With big radio telescopes. The radio telescopes listen for signals from space. Each day the Earth gives off billions of signals. Maybe aliens on other planets give off signals, too. These telescopes pick up all kinds of signals. They pick up many, many signals. Then computers sort through them. They look for any that did not come from Earth.

Why do we want to know if there are aliens? Because we want to know if we are alone. After all, ours is just one planet going around one star. That star is the sun. But there are 400 billion other stars just in our galaxy. And there are billions of other galaxies. That's why it's hard to believe that we are alone.

Hello! Anybody Out There? *(cont.)*

Directions: Answer these questions. You may look at the story.

1. How many galaxies are there besides our own?

   a. millions

   b. billions

   c. thousands

2. Why do scientists use radio telescopes?

   a. to take pictures of aliens

   b. to listen for alien signals

   c. to send signals to aliens

3. What does the word *alien* usually mean?

   _____

   _____

   _____

4. What do we know for sure about aliens?

   _____

   _____

   _____

5. How does the sun relate to the Earth?

   _____

   _____

   _____

6. Why do you think people want to look for aliens?

   _____

   _____

   _____

7. Do you think there are aliens in the universe? Explain.

   _____

   _____

   _____

Hello! Anybody Out There? *(cont.)*

Look at this movie poster.

Why do you think the artist chose to make the aliens look like this?

_____

_____

_____

_____

Welcome, Baby Panda!

The people at the San Diego Zoo in California are excited. Their giant panda had a baby! The cub weighed just four ounces. That's about as much as a stick of butter! She was born with white fuzz. She will get her black and white fur after a month. The cub was also born blind. She cannot open her eyes until she is about 45 days old.

This was the giant panda's first baby. People hoped that she would know how to take care of it. She had to feed it and keep it warm. The giant panda weighs 216 pounds. She had to be sure not to crush her cub by stepping or sitting on it. Worried zoo workers watched the panda on video 24 hours a day. What they saw made them happy. The panda knew just what to do. She fed and held her cub. She did not step or sit on her.

No wonder the workers were worried! There are fewer than 1,000 pandas left in the world. That is why one zoo worker thinks the cub's name should be Gift of Heaven.

Welcome, Baby Panda! *(cont.)*

Directions: Answer these questions. You may look at the story.

1. Where was the baby panda born?

    a. in China

    b. in a forest

    c. in California

2. Why did the zoo workers watch the pandas on video?

    a. They wanted to be sure the mother took good care of its cub.

    b. They wanted to make a movie of the cub.

    c. They were bored.

3. What were the workers worried about?

    _____

    _____

    _____

4. Why does the author write about a stick of butter?

    _____

    _____

    _____

5. How is a baby panda different from an adult panda?

    _____

    _____

    _____

6. Why did the zoo worker want to name the panda cub Gift of Heaven?

    _____

    _____

    _____

7. Do you think Gift of Heaven is a good name for the cub? Explain.

    _____

    _____

    _____

Welcome, Baby Panda! *(cont.)*

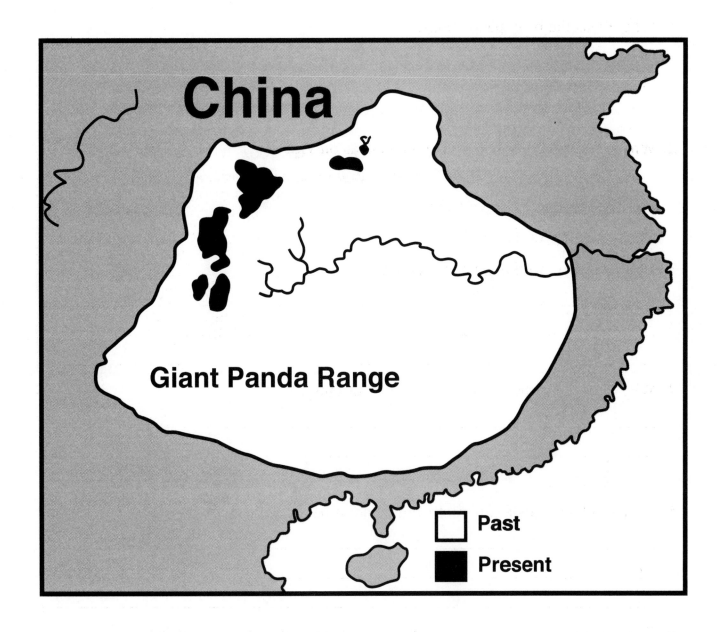

Look at the map. Why are scientists worried about the giant panda?

_____

_____

_____

_____

Saving the Day

All over the world, rescue groups help people after disasters. Hurricanes, floods, and fires are disasters. Disasters can hurt or kill people. They may ruin homes and buildings, too. When a disaster happens, rescue workers rush to help. They put their own lives in danger to save others. One of the oldest rescue groups is the Red Cross. It has helped people for more than 100 years.

There was an earthquake in Asia. Buildings fell down. A six-year-old boy got trapped. He was under a building. He was buried for more than three days. He needed air, water, and food. Workers did not stop until they reached him. They saved the little boy.

Saving the Day (cont.)

Directions: Answer these questions. You may look at the story.

1. How long was the boy buried?

    a. six hours

    b. one week

    c. three days

2. Why are disasters always bad?

    a. because they injure people and wreck things

    b. because they are not exciting

    c. because they are a surprise

3. What natural events are often disasters?

    _____

    _____

    _____

4. Why is rescue work dangerous?

    _____

    _____

    _____

5. Why did the workers need to reach the boy quickly?

    _____

    _____

    _____

6. How do you think that the workers felt when they reached the boy?

    _____

    _____

    _____

7. How do you think the boy felt while he was trapped? Explain.

    _____

    _____

    _____

Saving the Day *(cont.)*

The Earth is made up of many big, big plates. These plates meet at fault lines. When a plate moves at a fault line, it makes the ground shake. The point where the movement occurs is called the epicenter. The quake is felt for many miles around that point.

Look at this diagram. It shows what happens during an earthquake.

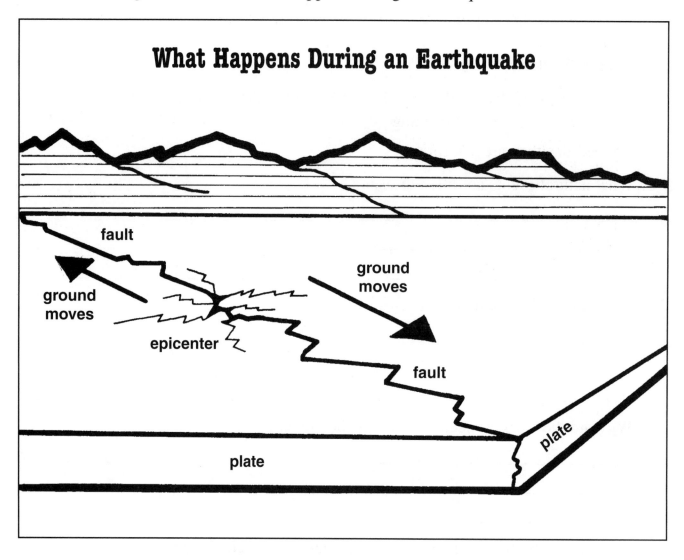

In the story a little boy was trapped under a building. On the diagram above, draw where you think the building stood before the quake. Using words from the diagram, explain why you think it was there.

_____

_____

_____

_____

Police Officer Next Door

Ellis Sinclair is a police officer. The police in his city wanted kids to stay out of trouble. So Sinclair moved into a house in a tough neighborhood.

He lives near 33 kids. Sinclair meets with these kids and their principal often. He listens to the kids whenever they need to talk. And things are getting better. Before he moved in, most of the kids had had problems with the law. Now only a few have had problems.

Sinclair says that this is much more than a job. He wants all of the kids to have a better life. He feels like they are his family. He really loves his job!

Police Officer Next Door *(cont.)*

Directions: Answer these questions. You may look at the story.

1. What is Ellis Sinclair?

    a. a father

    b. a principal

    c. a police officer

2. Why did Sinclair move next to the kids?

    a. to keep them healthy

    b. to keep them out of trouble

    c. to keep them safe from fires

3. Has Sinclair living in the tough neighborhood made any difference?

    _____

    _____

    _____

4. Why does Sinclair think of these kids as his family?

    _____

    _____

    _____

5. What do you think Sinclair and the principal talk about?

    _____

    _____

    _____

6. How does it help kids to have Sinclair live in their neighborhood?

    _____

    _____

    _____

7. Would you like Ellis Sinclair to live next door to you? Explain.

    _____

    _____

    _____

Police Officer Next Door (cont.)

This is a note that Officer Sinclair received.

How do you think most kids feel about having Officer Sinclair live there? Explain.

_____

_____

_____

_____

Honor at Last

Henry Flipper was born in 1856. He was a slave. But when he grew up, he went to a famous school. He was the first black man to go there. The school is West Point. West Point is an Army College. It is in New York. Many important U.S. leaders have gone to school there.

Henry Flipper was glad to be at West Point. He even wrote a book about his time there. He was proud to be in the army. But in 1881, an officer said that Flipper had taken $2,500. Flipper did not take the money. He had done nothing bad. He was found not guilty. But people said he had not acted like a good soldier. So he had to leave the army. He did not have a choice.

President Clinton signed a pardon for Flipper in 1999. The pardon said that Flipper had done nothing wrong. He should have stayed in the army. By then Flipper was dead. But his family watched President Clinton sign. They are glad that he got honor at last.

Honor at Last (cont.)

Directions: Answer these questions. You may look at the story.

1. Who was Henry Flipper?

    a. a soldier

    b. a teacher

    c. a president

2. Why did he leave the army?

    a. He didn't like it.

    b. He got old.

    c. People said he'd done a bad thing.

3. How long after Flipper left the army was he pardoned?

    _____

    _____

    _____

4. What happened after Flipper left the army?

    _____

    _____

    _____

5. How did Flipper probably feel when he left the army?

    _____

    _____

    _____

6. Why do you think President Clinton pardoned Flipper?

    _____

    _____

    _____

7. Is this story a happy one or a sad one? Why?

    _____

    _____

    _____

Honor at Last *(cont.)*

Today at West Point there is a bust (statue) of Henry Flipper's head. Under it is this sign.

Henry Ossian Flipper

1856-1940

U.S. Military Graduate of West Point

Class of 1877

First black graduate of West Point

Why does Henry Flipper have a bust and sign at West Point?

_____

_____

_____

_____

Elephants Talk to Her

Scientist Katy Payne listens to elephants. She uses a tape recorder. A tape catches what they "say." Then she plays the tape so others can hear the "voices," too. She went to Africa to hear the sounds made by wild elephants. She spent seven years there.

Katy started out studying how whales "talk" to each other. Whales use sounds to send messages to other whales. These whales are far away. Elephants do the same thing. But whales put their sounds together in a pattern. Elephants use each sound separately. What do the elephants say? They tell where they are. Katy says, "I think they mean, 'We're over here'."

Today elephants are in danger. They have been killed for their tusks. They have been crowded out of their homes. People should know how they talk. Then Katy thinks that more people would want to save them. "Elephants will speak for themselves, if you give them a chance," she says.

Elephants Talk to Her (cont.)

Directions: Answer these questions. You may look at the story.

1. What does Katy Payne study?

    a. sharks

    b. elephants

    c. monkeys

2. What does Katy believe elephants "say"?

    a. They tell each other where they are.

    b. They tell each other where to find food.

    c. They tell each other where to find water.

3. Besides using a tape recorder, how else could Katy Payne prove that elephants "talk"?

    _____

    _____

    _____

4. Why does Katy Payne want people to know that elephants "talk"?

    _____

    _____

    _____

5. Besides elephants, what other animals "talk" to each other?

    _____

    _____

    _____

6. Based on the story, what do elephants need to be safe?

    _____

    _____

    _____

7. What kind of animal would you like to study? Why? Explain.

    _____

    _____

    _____

Elephants Talk to Her *(cont.)*

Read this part of a report written by an elementary school student.

Wolves live in groups. They "talk" to each other. They do this by howling. Often more than one wolf howls at a time. Each group has its own area of land. They want other wolves to stay off their land. So, they howl to tell other wolves to stay away. They use other howls to say different things. They can howl to call to stray group members. Their howls may gather the group members for a hunt or warn of danger. They may even howl just because they are happy!

What do people, elephants, whales, and wolves have in common? Tell at least two ways they are alike.

_____

_____

_____

_____

A Very Cool Hotel

How would you like to sleep on a bed of ice? What would you think if someone said to you, "Welcome to our hotel. Come on in where it's cold!"?

That is what happens at the Ice Hotel. The Ice Hotel is in a town in Sweden. Both the hotel and the beds are made completely out of ice and snow. The room temperature is just 20°F. That is 12 degrees below freezing. Brrr! The guests keep warm by covering up with reindeer skins. Their beds are covered with reindeer skins, too.

Why would people want to stay at an ice hotel? Why would people want to sleep on top of a big ice cube? The manager says, "People enjoy the beauty. It is pure winter. It is white and fresh snow and total quiet." The 4,000 people who stay there each year must agree.

Each spring the Ice Hotel melts. It turns into a big puddle. But by the next October, builders start making a new one.

A Very Cool Hotel _(cont.)_

Directions: Answer these questions. You may look at the story.

1. Where is the Ice Hotel?

    a. Sweden

    b. Switzerland

    c. Alaska

2. Why do guests sleep on reindeer skins?

    a. to keep from getting too warm

    b. to keep from getting too cold

    c. to make the bed more firm

3. Why does the Ice Hotel melt in the spring?

    _____

    _____

    _____

4. How does the Ice Hotel differ from regular hotels?

    _____

    _____

    _____

5. What does the Ice Hotel most remind you of?

    _____

    _____

    _____

6. What must the hotel's guests like?

    _____

    _____

    _____

7. Should the Ice Hotel add a swimming pool? Explain.

    _____

    _____

    _____

Read this poem.

Ice Town

What if the town were made all of ice?

The buildings all shiny,

slippery, and nice.

The streets filled with music,

sound bouncing around,

while kids in ice skates spun on the ground.

We'd wear visors to save us

from the bright glare.

There would be no cars,

just cold, clean, crisp air.

A place to cuddle close, freezing but fun . . .

Until the town melted away

in the warm springtime sun.

—-Katrina Housel

Do you think that the writer of this poem would like to visit the Ice Hotel? Explain.

_____

_____

_____

_____

Antarctic Shipwreck!

Captain Shackleton and his crew seemed ready for anything. The captain and 27 men packed food, tents, and warm clothes on their ship. Their ship was the *Endurance.* In 1914, these men hoped to be the first to go all of the way across Antarctica. They did not make it. But they did make history. They lived through a big adventure.

The *Endurance* sailed for Antarctica. When it was just 100 miles away, ice closed in around it. The ship could not go forward. The ship could not go back. It just could not move! The big ship stayed stuck for 10 months. Then the ice started to crush the ship. The captain made the men get off. Most of the men stayed on cold, icy Elephant Island. But the captain and five men rowed away in a tiny rowboat. They rowed 800 miles in stormy seas. Four months later, the captain came back for his crew. He was glad to see that everyone had survived! How? Because Captain Shackleton was a good leader. As he said, "If you're a leader, you've got to keep going."

Antarctic Shipwreck! *(cont.)*

Directions: Answer these questions. You may look at the story.

1. Where did this adventure take place?

   a. near Antarctica

   b. near Australia

   c. in the Arctic Ocean

2. How long did the adventure last?

   a. more than one year

   b. exactly one year

   c. less than one year

3. Why was *Endurance* a good name for this ship?

   _____

   _____

   _____

4. Why didn't the captain send a letter to get help?

   _____

   _____

   _____

5. Why did the captain go for help himself rather than sending others?

   _____

   _____

   _____

6. Why did the captain and his crew want to be the first to make it across Antarctica?

   _____

   _____

   _____

7. How is the shipwreck of the *Endurance* different from most shipwrecks? Tell at least two ways.

   _____

   _____

   _____

Antarctic Shipwreck! *(cont.)*

Read this death notice for Captain Shackleton.

January 8, 1922

SHACKLETON, Ernest. Age 47. Struck down by a heart attack on January 5th near South Georgia Island on his way to Antarctica. Survived by his beloved wife Emily and three children. Knighted in 1909. Sir Shackleton accompanied Robert Scott's trip to Antarctica (1901-1904). He then led his own group (1908-1909). On a third trip, his ship, the *Endurance*, was stranded by ice, but his entire crew survived. He wrote *Heart of the Antarctic* (1909) and *South* (1919). Burial at Whaler's Cemetery in Grytviken, South Georgia.

What really interested Captain Shackleton? How do you know?

_____

_____

_____

_____

The Fossil Finder

Long ago an animal died. It fell to the ground. Mud covered it. Over time more mud pressed down on it. After a very long time its bones changed into rock. This rock is called a fossil.

Many scientists look for fossils. They find them in very old rocks. Some are millions of years old. Many of the fossil animals and plants have died off. They are no longer here. The only way to know about them is by their fossils.

When Sam Girouard was 8 years old, he went to see his grandmother. She lived in Alabama. There they explored an old mine. What they found inside changed Sam's life. "It was just packed with fossils," says Sam. Sam has been looking for fossils ever since. The teenager is now a fossil scientist. He helped to dig up a T Rex skeleton. He has also found a mastodon bone. A mastodon looked like an elephant. Its bone was more than 4 million years old!

Sam doesn't tell other scientists his age right away. "I'm afraid that if people knew my age, my work would not be taken seriously," he says.

The Fossil Finder *(cont.)*

Directions: Answer these questions. You may look at the story.

1. Where are fossils often found?

    a. in old rocks

    b. in old buildings

    c. in old boxes

2. How old was the mastodon bone Sam found?

    a. thousands of years

    b. millions of years

    c. billions of years

3. How long has Sam been a fossil hunter?

    _____

    _____

    _____

4. Since they no longer exist, how do we know about dinosaurs?

    _____

    _____

    _____

5. Why might Sam's age bother some scientists?

    _____

    _____

    _____

6. How did Sam's life change at the age of 8?

    _____

    _____

    _____

7. Do you think looking for fossils sounds like fun? Explain.

    _____

    _____

    _____

The Fossil Finder *(cont.)*

Fossil Time Line
Dates Are Millions of Years Ago

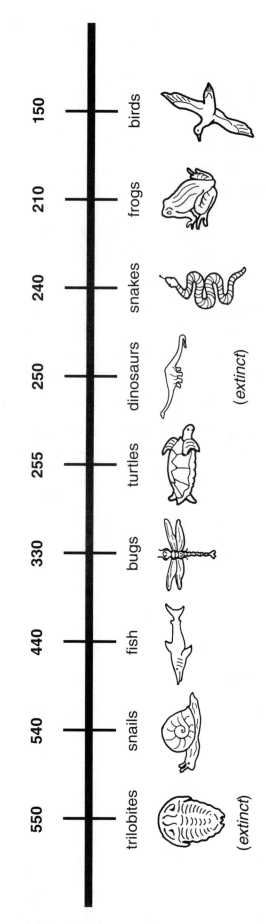

150	210	240	250	255	330	440	540	550
birds	frogs	snakes	dinosaurs	turtles	bugs	fish	snails	trilobites
			(extinct)					*(extinct)*

(Extinct means they are no longer here.)

How have fossils made this time line possible?

_____

_____

_____

_____

Directions: Read the story.

Great Ball of Fire!

The sun seems like a quiet neighbor. It gives us heat. It gives us light. It makes plants grow. It never makes any noise. But the sun isn't really quiet. It is really a big ball of burning gas! It is so bright that if we look right at it, we could go blind. The temperature in the middle of the sun is 57 million degrees Fahrenheit. It is bigger than one million of our Earths! Yet next to some other stars, its temperature and size are average.

The sun has solar wind. Solar wind is tiny bits of hot gas that come from its surface. These pieces fly through the solar system. They affect our weather. Solar storms blow across the sun's surface. These storms can cause trouble. Compasses stop working. Electric power gets knocked out. Phones do not work.

Scientists need to know more about the sun. They want to study its storms and wind. They want to be able to predict solar weather. They want to know all about the sun's effects on the Earth. So in 1997 they sent up a telescope. It has been going around and around the sun. It has been taking pictures. It has been taking measurements. Now scientists will know more about the sun than ever before.

Great Ball of Fire! *(cont.)*

Directions: Answer these questions. You may look at the story.

1. What gives our Earth heat and light?

    a. the stars

    b. the moon

    c. the sun

2. When was the telescope sent up?

    a. more than 100 years ago

    b. more than 5 years ago

    c. last year

3. Which is the biggest, the Earth, the moon or the sun?

    _____

    _____

    _____

4. Why do you think scientists want to know more about the sun?

    _____

    _____

5. Why would the sun's effect on compasses be a problem for hikers?

    _____

    _____

6. During a solar storm, will you probably be able to watch TV? Explain.

    _____

    _____

7. Do you think that someday people will be able to walk on our sun? Explain.

    _____

    _____

    _____

Great Ball of Fire! *(cont.)*

Read this page from a science textbook. Look at the illustration.

Science Today   *Chapter 4: Our Earth*

The Equator divides the Earth in half. So, Earth has a top half and a bottom half. The top half is called the Northern Hemisphere. It lies above the Equator. The bottom half is called the Southern Hemisphere. It lies below the Equator.

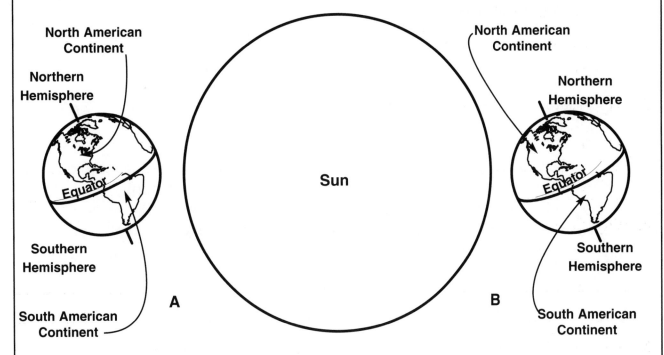

The seasons in the two hemispheres are always the opposite. When one has fall, the other has spring. The seasons change when the amount of sunlight falling on each hemisphere changes. The part of the Earth tipped toward the sun gets the most sunlight. It is warm. At the same time the other part of the Earth is tipped away from the sun. It gets less sunlight. So, it is cold.

page 165

Does A or B show the Northern Hemisphere in summer?_____

Does A or B show the Southern Hemisphere in summer?_____

How do you know?

_____

_____

China's Dam is a Good Idea

The Yangtze (*Yang*-see) River in China is beautiful. Lots of water flows through it. But it has had bad floods. These floods have killed many people. The floods have ruined homes and crops. Now a new dam will stop these floods. This dam will also turn the water's energy into electricity. Its name is the Three Gorges Dam.

In 1997, the work was started. Bulldozers dumped rocks into the river. They started to block the river. The river is the third longest in the world. So the dam will not be done until 2009. When it is done, it will be the biggest dam in the world.

Some people are upset about the dam. They don't like the big lake that will form behind it. This lake will cover up their homes. They don't want to move away. Others worry that the big lake will cover the homes of animals like giant pandas. But the dam will do more good than harm. People need the electricity. And with no dam, those who must move are in danger from floods if they stay where they are. There is still a lot of land for the animals' homes. The dam is a good thing for China.

China's Dam is a Good Idea *(cont.)*

Directions: Answer these questions. You may look at the story.

1. When did they start building the Three Gorges Dam?

    a. 1997

    b. 2000

    c. 2009

2. How long do they think it will take to finish the dam?

    a. 5 years

    b. 10 years

    c. 13 years

3. What happened before the Yangtze River dam was built?

    _____

    _____

    _____

4. Why is the dam a good idea?

    _____

    _____

    _____

5. How will the dam cause problems?

    _____

    _____

    _____

6. What will be changed forever as a result of the Three Gorges Dam?

    _____

    _____

    _____

7. Do you think that the dam is a good idea? Explain.

    _____

    _____

    _____

China's Dam is a Good Idea *(cont.)*

This cut-away diagram shows how the Three Gorges Dam will make electric power.

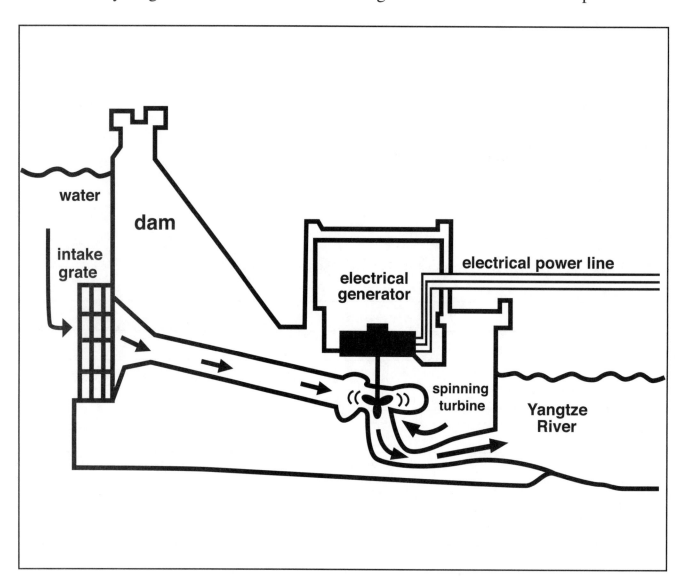

Why do you think there is a grate over the water intake? Explain.

_____

_____

_____

_____

Pooh Stays!

They are old and worn. But they are loved a lot. Who are they? The first Winnie-the-Pooh and his friends. His friends are Tigger, Eeyore, Kanga, and Piglet. These toys are in a New York City library. They stay in a glass case.

How did Pooh and his friends get there? In the 1920s these toys were in Britain. They belonged to a little boy. His name was Christopher Robin Milne. His father thought up stories about these toys. He wrote the Pooh books. These books were published in New York City. The book publisher gave the toys to the library.

In 1998, a lawmaker in Britain was upset. She wanted the toys to be in Britain. She asked the library to send them back. "They look very unhappy," she said. "We want our Winnie-the-Pooh back, along with all of his friends!"

But the New York City mayor wanted them to stay where they are. "They have been very happy here," he said.

Pooh Stays! *(cont.)*

Directions: Answer these questions. You may look at the story.

1. Who was Christopher Robin Milne?

   a. the person who gave the toys to the library

   b. the man who wrote the Pooh stories

   c. the boy who first owned Pooh

2. What is Winnie-the-Pooh?

   a. a stuffed toy donkey

   b. a stuffed toy kangaroo

   c. a stuffed toy bear

3. What happened after Pooh and his friends were given to the library?

   _____

   _____

   _____

4. Why do some people feel that the Pooh toys should be in Britain?

   _____

   _____

   _____

5. Why do you think the toys are kept in a glass case?

   _____

   _____

   _____

6. Does the New York City mayor think the toys are valuable? Why?

   _____

   _____

   _____

7. Do you think Pooh and his friends should go back to Britain? Explain.

   _____

   _____

   _____

Pooh Stays! *(cont.)*

Look at these pictures to fill in the chart.

Bear

Winnie-the-Pooh

Ways Pooh Is Like a Real Bear	Ways Pooh Is Not Like a Real Bear

After the Spill

In March 1989, a big ship crashed near Alaska. The ship was the *Exxon Valdez*. When it hit some rocks, it spilled lots of oil into the sea. This spill was one of the worst ever. It was big news. It took years to clean up the mess. It took more than 10,000 workers.

Ten years later a report came out. It told what had happened to animals after the spill. The spill had hurt many animals. Their homes and food were covered with oil. A lot of them died. Twenty-two whales, 300 seals, and 3,000 otters were killed. The spill left many birds covered in oil. So 250,000 seabirds died, too.

Now there is both good news and bad news. The otters and eagles are coming back. So are the salmon and clams. But the seals, ducks, and whales are not. Things may never be the same again.

After the Spill *(cont.)*

Directions: Answer these questions. You may look at the story.

1. How many people did it take to clean up the spill?

   a. about 1,000

   b. about 10,000

   c. about 100,000

2. What is the *Exxon Valdez* the name of?

   a. a ship

   b. an island

   c. a disaster

3. What animals had the most deaths from the spill?

   _____

   _____

   _____

4. Which animals are having trouble coming back?

   _____

   _____

   _____

5. Why do you think that the author wrote about a crash that happened over ten years ago?

   _____

   _____

   _____

6. How might things be forever changed by the spill?

   _____

   _____

   _____

7. How is an oil spill like a forest fire? Explain.

   _____

   _____

   _____

After the Spill *(cont.)*

Major Oil Spills
in chronological order

Year	Where	Millions of Gallons	Cause
1978	Brittany coast	68	shipwreck
1979	Gulf of Mexico	140	off-shore oil well blew up
1989	Alaskan coast	10	ship hit underwater rocks
1989	Canary Islands	19	ship blew up
1991	Persian Gulf	460	dumped on purpose during the Persian Gulf War
1994	Russia	5	oil dam burst, spilling into a nearby river
1996	Welsh coast	5	shipwreck

Look at the chart. List the places in which there were bigger spills than the *Exxon Valdez*.

_____

_____

_____

_____

Long, Tall Dino

Matt Wedel has made an exciting discovery. He found the tallest dinosaur yet. It was 60 feet tall. That is as tall as a six-story building. Now imagine you are on the sixth floor of a building. You look out the window. You are looking right into a big eye. It's the eye of a big dinosaur! How would you feel?

The new dinosaur is named sauroposeidon (saw-ro-po-*sy*-den). Its name comes from the Greek god of the sea and earthquakes. That's because sauroposeidon made the ground shake when it walked. It weighed 60 tons. Next to it, a person would look like a bug!

In 1999, scientists showed the dinosaur's neck bones. Its neck was as long as a school bus! Parts of these neck bones were very thin. They were as thin as eggshells. Why? Because if the bones had been heavy, the dinosaur could not have lifted its head!

Long, Tall Dino *(cont.)*

Directions: Answer these questions. You may look at the story.

1. About how tall is sauroposeidon?

    a. as tall as a school bus

    b. as tall as a Greek god

    c. as tall as the sixth floor of a building

2. Why did sauroposeidon have thin, light neck bones?

    a. It needed to lift its head.

    b. It needed to lay eggs.

    c. It was so tall.

3. Why did the new dinosaur remind scientists of the Greek god?

    _____

    _____

    _____

4. How many dinosaurs are even taller than sauroposeidon?

    _____

    _____

    _____

5. Why do you think sauroposeidon was tall?

    _____

    _____

    _____

6. What might an elephant have looked like next to a sauroposeidon?

    _____

    _____

    _____

7. If you could, would you like to see a living dinosaur? Explain.

    _____

    _____

    _____

Long, Tall Dino *(cont.)*

Sauroposeidon is named after the Greek god Poseidon (Po-*sy*-den). There are many other Greek gods. One of them is Hermes (Her-*meez*). He has wings on his golden sandals.   He is the god of speed because he carries messages so fast. Hermes always moves quickly and smoothly.

Think of an animal that reminds you of Hermes. Tell the name of the animal and explain how it is like Hermes.

_____

_____

_____

_____

Directions: Read the story.

Puerto Rico: The 51ˢᵗ State

Nine hundred miles south of Miami is a beautiful island. The island is Puerto Rico. It is a part of the U.S. It was given to the U.S. at the end of the Spanish-American War. So, its people are American citizens. But they cannot vote. Puerto Rico sends a person to the U.S. Congress. But that person cannot vote.

Why? Because Puerto Rico is not a state. If it were a state, the people would vote. They would vote for leaders. They would vote for laws. They would have a say in the government. That is why so many people there want it to be a state. But others do not want it to be. They are afraid. They say that Puerto Rico may lose its language. They fear that Puerto Rico will lose its customs. They do not want that to happen.

Puerto Ricans are American citizens. They should have the right to vote. Puerto Rico should be a state.

Puerto Rico: The 51ˢᵗ State *(cont.)*

Directions: Answer these questions. You may look at the story.

1. Where is Puerto Rico?

    a. in South America

    b. south of Miami

    c. north of Miami

2. What makes Puerto Ricans different from most American citizens?

    a. They cannot vote.

    b. They cannot drive.

    c. They cannot leave their island.

3. How would things change for the people on the island if Puerto Rico became a state?

    _____

    _____

    _____

4. Why do Puerto Ricans send a person to Congress?

    _____

    _____

    _____

5. Why do you think Puerto Rico was given to the U.S.?

    _____

    _____

    _____

6. Why do many people want Puerto Rico to be a state?

    _____

    _____

    _____

7. Do you think it is a good idea for Puerto Rico to become the 51ˢᵗ state? Explain.

    _____

    _____

    _____

Puerto Rico: The 51ˢᵗ State *(cont.)*

Look at the flags. Then fill in the chart.

This is the Puerto Rican flag.

There are three red stripes,
two white stripes, a white star,
and a blue triangle.

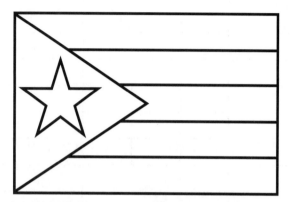

This is the American flag.

There are seven red stripes,
six white stripes, a blue rectangle,
and fifty white stars.

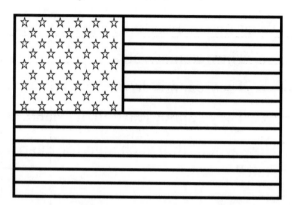

How the Puerto Rican Flag Is Similar to the American Flag	How the Puerto Rican Flag Is Different from the American Flag

Student Achievement Graph

Passage Title	Number of Questions Correctly Answered							
	1	2	3	4	5	6	7	8

Answer Key

Page 17
1. b
2. c
3. Many people thought that it was too small to be a Great Lake.
4. Yes, now they would get money to study it.
5. the effects of pollution on the fish in the lakes
6. They can use it for drinking, washing, watering plants, etc.
7. Allow reasonable and supported responses.

Page 18
Answers may vary but will likely say that, no, Lake Champlain should not be a Great Lake. It is too small, and it is not connected to the other Great Lakes.

Page 20
1. c
2. b
3. Ankylosaurs were here long before scientists thought they were.
4. Answers may vary.
5. Answers may vary but may state that there are probably still more new dinosaurs to find.
6. The nodosaurid had shoulder spikes; the ankylosaurid didn't.
7. Allow reasonable and supported responses.

Page 21
Allow reasonable responses such as, "I could learn how the dinosaurs lived, hunted, and ate."

Page 23
1. b
2. a
3. Moondust starts to circle the planet.
4. Answers may vary but the best answer is rings of moondust
5. The writer tells us that Jupiter is two times bigger than Earth.
6. Answers will vary.
7. Allow reasonable and supported responses.

Page 24
A new moon is when the moon is not visible. It is totally in shadow. A full moon is when the whole moon is seen. None of it is in shadow.

Page 26
1. a
2. b
3. The bus would have crashed.
4. Answers may vary but the best answer is "to tell us about a kid who did the right thing."
5. because he saved kids from getting hurt; because he was a hero
6. Answers will vary.
7. Allow reasonable and supported responses.

Page 27
Allow yes or no as long as the opinion is supported.

Page 29
1. b
2. a
3. She was afraid of the coming tornado and thought she might not be able to outrun it.
4. They would have been hit by hail.
5. so the reader could picture how big the pieces were
6. Answers will vary but will likely suggest "under a bridge."
7. Allow reasonable and supported responses.

Page 30
These places are the safest because they are all low. It is good to be by an inside wall in case the outside walls blow away.

Page 32
1. c
2. b
3. how to do magic
4. They are so popular.
5. He is a wizard.
6. Answers will vary.
7. Allow reasonable and supported responses.

Page 33
Sarah Grayfield has a flying carpet, and she may meet a lake monster and a giant eagle. She may have an adventure with a wizard and a treasure chest.

Page 35
1. a
2. a
3. because their boats get stuck in the plants
4. all
5. Water hyacinths were clogging Lake Victoria.
6. They want to get rid of them.
7. Allow reasonable and supported responses such as, "The Swamp Devil solves the problem more quickly."

Page 36
Both are aliens that accidentally got into these lakes. They are both harming the lakes' ecosystems.

Page 38
1. b
2. b
3. She would have died.
4. They will take care of it and put it back into the ocean.
5. Answers may vary but will likely suggest that they were glad she was going where she belonged.
6. No, it is her home and other whales will help her.
7. Allow reasonable and supported responses.

Page 39
People like to see whales at water parks because they are entertaining. They do tricks for the people. It is also one of the few chances people ever have to see a living whale up close.

Page 41
1. b
2. a
3. b
4. to describe the sound of walking in really cold snow
5. They don't want them to get frostbite.
6. Answers will vary but should state things related to putting oneself in danger from the bitter cold (such as going outdoors unprotected).
7. Allow reasonable and supported responses.

Page 42
It was colder in Alaska in 1971. The lowest temperatures are both in Alaska because it has the harshest winter and is the farthest north of all the U.S. states.

Page 44
1. c
2. c
3. so she could play on the equipment with her friends
4. He or she has a hard time getting out of the chair and using the equipment.
5. Answers will vary but can include a wide variety of responses, including things such as she can play, love, eat, laugh, have feelings, think, etc.
6. Yes, of course.
7. Allow reasonable and supported responses.

Page 45
The Paralympics are important to someone like Hannah because they prove that disabled people can succeed at many of the same things that other people can.

Page 47
1. a
2. c
3. People have been making music for at least 33,000 years.
4. They want to know how the people lived.
5. The people played music.
6. Answers may vary but will likely suggest they were excited to learn that people long ago liked music.
7. Allow reasonable and supported responses such as music cheered them up and helped them to celebrate.

Page 48
The other instruments ancient people played were mouth organs, harps, drums, oboes, and string instruments.

Answer Key *(cont.)*

Page 50
1. b
2. a
3. coins and jewelry
4. valuable things
5. Answers may vary but the best answer is "to tell about the people buried there."
6. Answers may vary but will likely suggest that the mummies may have been kings or queens.
7. Allow reasonable and supported responses.

Page 51
Allow reasonable and supported responses.

Page 53
1. c
2. b
3. about 50 feet
4. Nobody has ever studied one that was still alive.
5. an octopus
6. No, giant squids are rarely seen, and they live in deep water.
7. Allow reasonable and supported responses.

Page 54
The price is free. The museum wants kids to have the opportunity to see the giant squid. If it was not free, some kids might not be able to go.

Page 56
1. c
2. a
3. They are prey for the tigers.
4. Answers should include home, food, and/or safety from hunters.
5. The tigers live in a place with laws against hunting.
6. There might get to be too many of them.
7. Allow reasonable and supported responses such as, "The deer and wild boar were disappearing for probably the same reasons that the tigers were disappearing: a lack of homes and overhunting."

Page 57
Yes, the writer of the poem says that we should help the tigers, and the law would help more tigers live.

Page 59
1. c
2. a
3. bad weather, getting lost, landing in the sea, or running into something
4. It is always cold high in the sky.
5. Answers will vary.
6. Answers will vary but may suggest that the person who makes history has done something that no one else has ever done before.
7. Allow reasonable and supported responses.

Page 60
Probably most sightings happen at night when people cannot see very clearly. Planes are the most common things flying in the sky, which is why most UFO sightings turn out to be planes.

Page 62
1. a
2. a
3. She started playing when she was young and she is a good athlete.
4. They wanted to show that they were the best at tennis.
5. Answers will vary but may likely suggest racquetball, ping-pong, or badminton.
6. Answers will vary. "Champion sisters" is a good idea.
7. Allow reasonable and supported responses such as, "Most games have a winner and a loser, rules, a ball, something to hit the ball with, and a special playing field."

Page 63
Allow reasonable and supported responses such as Kameela wanted to let Serena know how much she admires her.

Page 65
1. b
2. b
3. from another place
4. We don't know anything for sure.
5. The Earth goes around the sun.
6. Answers will vary but may state that they want to find out if aliens are real.
7. Allow reasonable and supported responses.

Page 66
The artist made the aliens on the poster look like the ones that are in the movie.

Page 68
1. c
2. a
3. that the mother bear would step on or sit on her cub
4. so the reader can picture the newborn cub's size
5. Answers will vary but should state that a panda is born blind.
6. because the cub is so rare
7. Allow reasonable and supported responses.

Page 69
Scientists are worried because the giant panda has very few places left in which to live.

Page 71
1. c
2. a
3. Answers may include earthquakes, tornadoes, hurricanes, monsoons, etc.
4. The rescuers may end up in the same trouble from which they are trying to rescue others. They often put themselves in danger, too.
5. He was running out of air and needed food and water.
6. Answers will vary but will probably suggest they were glad because the boy was alive.
7. Allow reasonable and supported responses.

Page 72
The building should be drawn near the fault line, preferably near the epicenter. The earthquake is strongest at the epicenter, and all along the fault line the ground shifts and buildings fall down.

Page 74
1. c
2. b
3. Yes, fewer kids get in trouble with the law.
4. He really cares about them.
5. Answers should suggest they talk about the kids, their schoolwork, school attendance, or school behavior.
6. Answers will vary but may suggest that the kids have someone to whom they can talk and admire as a role model.
7. Allow reasonable and supported responses.

Page 75
Most of the kids probably like having Officer Sinclair there. Jose Ortiz even wrote him a note saying so. And crime is going down among the kids in the area.

Page 77
1. a
2. c
3. more than 100 years
4. We don't know what happened in his life, but long after his death he was pardoned by President Clinton
5. unhappy or angry
6. Answers will vary but will probably suggest that he wanted to make it clear that Flipper was innocent.
7. Allow reasonable and supported responses.

Page 78
West Point is proud of Henry Flipper. He was the first black American to graduate from West Point.

Page 80
1. b
2. a
3. by recording them on videotape
4. because then more people will care about the elephants
5. whales
6. a place to live where hunters cannot kill them
7. Allow reasonable and supported responses.

Answer Key (cont.)

Page 81

People, elephants, whales, and wolves can communicate with their own kind. These animals are all mammals. They are warm-blooded and give birth to live babies. The babies drink their mothers' milk. They all have a spine and a skeleton. (Accept any two responses.)

Page 83

1. a
2. b
3. because the weather warms up
4. It is kept very cold and is made of ice.
5. Answers will vary but may state "an igloo."
6. Answers may suggest such things as winter, cold, and white.
7. Allow reasonable and supported responses such as, "No, the water would freeze in the pool."

Page 84

Yes, the writer sounds like she would like to visit an entire town made of ice.

Page 86

1. a
2. a
3. Answers may vary, but the best answer is because the crew had to endure being stranded for a long time.
4. He couldn't send mail from his ship.
5. He felt that he should put himself in the most danger.
6. Answers will vary. A good answer is that they wanted to see what they could accomplish.
7. The shipwreck was unusual because it took more than a year for the crew to be rescued. Everyone survived. It took place in a very cold, remote location. The ship was trapped by ice. (Accept any two responses.)

Page 87

Captain Shackleton was interested in Antarctica. He wrote two books about it and died on his fourth trip to Antarctica.

Page 89

1. a
2. b
3. most of his life
4. We have fossils from dinosaurs.
5. Answers may suggest that they will not take him seriously because he is so young.
6. He got interested in fossils.
7. Allow reasonable and supported responses.

Page 90

Fossils tell us when different kinds of animals appeared. They let us know about animals that are no longer here like trilobites and dinosaurs.

Page 92

1. c
2. b
3. the sun
4. Answers will vary.
5. They need a compass to work correctly in order to find their way in the wilderness.
6. Probably not, because a television is run by electricity and electricity can be affected by solar storms.
7. Allow reasonable and supported responses such as, "Probably not, due to the incredibly hot temperature of the sun."

Page 93

B shows the Northern Hemisphere in summer. A shows the Southern Hemisphere in summer. I know because that is when each hemisphere is tipped toward the sun.

Page 95

1. a
2. c
3. The Yangtze River flooded.
4. It will stop floods.
5. It will make some animals have to find new homes.
6. Answers may vary, but the best answer is the Yangtze River itself.
7. Allow reasonable and supported responses.

Page 96

The grate keeps things from getting caught in the turbine. If something hit the turbine, it could ruin it or jam it. Only when the turbine runs is electrical power made.

Page 98

1. c
2. c
3. A lawmaker in Britain asked for the toys back.
4. The toys first belonged to a boy who lived in Britain.
5. to keep them safe
6. Yes, because they're the real toys on which the Pooh stories are based.
7. Allow reasonable and supported responses.

Page 99

Pooh is like a real bear because he is shaped like a bear and has brown fur and movable limbs. Pooh is not like a real bear because he is not alive and does not breathe, eat, or sleep. His eyes, nose, and mouth are not real and are sewed on to his body.

Page 101

1. b
2. a
3. birds
4. seals, ducks, and whales
5. because the real results of the crash are finally known

6. Answers will vary but may state that there may be fewer whales, seals, and ducks than ever before.
7. An oil spill and a forest fire are alike because they ruin animals' homes and food supply and they kill many animals. It takes a long time for things to get back to normal.

Page 102

Four places had bigger spills: Brittany coast, Gulf of Mexico, Canary Islands, and the Persian Gulf.

Page 104

1. c
2. a
3. When it walked, it made the ground shake like an earthquake.
4. none
5. Answers will vary, but a good answer is so that it could reach the leaves at the tops of trees.
6. Answers will vary, but something like a mouse would be a good answer.
7. Allow reasonable and supported responses.

Page 105

Allow reasonable and supported responses for animals that run swiftly and gracefully (such as a cheetah) or have wings (such as an eagle).

Page 107

1. b
2. a
3. They would have a say in the government.
4. to know what is going on in the government
5. because Spain lost the war
6. Answers will vary, but the best answer should suggest they want to have a say about new laws.
7. Allow reasonable and supported responses.

Page 108

The Puerto Rican flag is like the U.S. flag because it has red and white stripes and a white star on a blue background. It is different because it has only one star, the blue area is shaped like a triangle, and it has fewer stripes.